THE ART OF
TITHING

15TH ANNIVERSARY EDITION

THE ART OF TITHING

Harness the Power of Giving Thanks & Create Lasting Inner and Outer Wealth

PAULA LANGGUTH RYAN

Foreword by Rev. Catherine Ponder
author of *Dynamic Laws of Prosperity*

MEDIA

MEDIA

Published 2021 by Gildan Media LLC
aka G&D Media
www.GandDmedia.com

Front cover design by David Rheinhardt of Pyrographx

Interior design by Meghan Day Healey of Story Horse, LLC

Library of Congress Cataloging-in-Publication Data is available upon request

ISBN: 978-1-7225-0563-9

10   9   8   7   6   5   4   3   2   1

*To everyone, everywhere,
whose life has ever touched mine.
You helped me prosper and grow in
untold ways. I dedicate this book to you,
with all my thanks. Thank you for
feeding my spirit and for allowing
me to feed yours.*

Testimonials

"The best book I've ever seen on the art of tithing."

—Joe Vitale, as seen in "The Secret"

& author of *Zero Limits*

"The world needs this book."

—Rev. Catherine Ponder, Unity Church Worldwide

"This was the final piece I was missing from the tithing puzzle. Thanks for bringing it together for me in a way no one else ever did!"

—Karen K., TN

"You write with such beautiful clarity . . . I was impressed . . . May [this book] do its part in removing the cloud of scarcity hovering over so many in our world today."

—John Randolph Price, Quartus Foundation

for Spiritual Research

"After reading your book, tithing finally made sense. You brought it to life and explained the mechanics of tithing in a way I've never read before. If every church in the country read and studied your book, they would explode in growth and that growth would register on the Richter Scale as a tremor! Thank you!"

—Greg Whitaker, Debt Shepherd

"Your material is excellent. It is clear, based on immutable spiritual principle and offers a way to move into the tithing experience."

—Blaine C. Mays, International
New Thought Alliance (INTA)

Contents

Foreword

The word "tithe" means "tenth" and since ancient times all great civilizations have taught the power of caring and sharing through the act of tithing a tenth of one's income at the point or points where one is being inspired.

Tithing has been described as "the permanent road to prosperity." I began tithing sixty years ago at a time when a tenth of my weekly income was $2.50.

This simple, weekly act brought gradual increase over the years. Tithing is not "a get rich quick scheme." It is a universal law endorsed by our Creator to help humankind prosper and succeed on all levels of life.

Of all the prosperity laws I have researched and written about in seventeen books, I receive more mail about the tithing law of prosperity than all the others combined! People are hungry to know of this divine and permanent law of prosperity.

So I invite you to join countless people worldwide as you "tithe and thrive." This book shows you how!

—Rev. Catherine Ponder, Author,

Dynamic Laws of Prosperity

Introduction

"If the only prayer you ever say is 'thank you,' it will suffice."
—MEISTER ECKHART

When I first wrote *Giving Thanks* (now newly released as *The Art of Tithing*) fifteen years ago, I had no idea it would become an internationally-acclaimed book, read by people in sixty-seven countries. Or that a lovely mother-daughter team would freely translate it into Spanish so *more* people could read it. Or that the incomparable Jim Lefter would gift the world with an ebook version so these teachings could reach even *more* people!

You're about to discover the truth about the level of abundance in your life. Your abundance—your prosperity, worth and value—has absolutely *nothing* to do with the balance in your bank account. It has *everything* to do with the amount of gratitude you have, and how open you are to both giving and receiving, with no strings attached.

In 2015 at the request of many churches and other organizations, I created a study guide to accompany the original book. Students found the study guide was both transformational *and* confusing.

In anticipation of releasing this 15th anniversary edition, I asked renowned literary agent and publishing coach Rachelle Gardner for guidance on how to make the study guide material more enjoyable and intuitive for you. The result is what you're reading now.

The 10-session *Tithing Mastery Study Guide* has been incorporated into this edition. I believe—whether you're reading on your own or with a group—this book will help you build a permanent foundation of financial peace and abundance in your life. I do encourage you to create a study group of friends, family or fellow travelers if possible to support you on your journey!

This book contains the precise formula you need to release old beliefs around giving and receiving. In writing this book, I used language that has meaning for me. Some words may simply not resonate with you, or may not have meaning for you. People keep telling me I'd sell many more copies if I remove the words *tithing* and *God*. The challenge is—for me—this is what giving and receiving is all about. So, you will find this book contains references to God. If that three-letter word is uncomfortable for you, I invite you to substitute Infinite Intelligence,

Source, Universe, Universal Energy, Great Spirit, Science, Goddess, Divine Love, or whatever else you feel comfortable calling the unexplained energy that swirls among us and created such wonders as human beings, dragonflies and the waves. It's all the same thing. It's all Good!

At the end of each chapter, you'll find Discussion Questions and Activities. When it comes to the discussion questions (especially as you get into the second half of the book) you may want to divide the questions up among groups of people, or have each person pick an "easy" question and a "hard" question to explore for themselves. If you come across a question where your immediate response is "NO WAY am I answering THAT question!" stop and consider it for just a moment. The questions that evoke the biggest resistance in us are usually the ones that will create the biggest transformation! For the first five weeks at least, answer all the questions and do all the activities.

This program revolves around two important universal laws: the *Law of Supply and Demand* and the *Divine Law of Prosperity*. I've included them below so you can commit them to memory.

Law of Supply and Demand: There is no limit to any supply. Until we have a specific demand, however, we never tap the proper supply.

Divine Law of Prosperity: Until you learn to be happy with what you have, you won't be happy with more. Universal abundance is unlimited and you can tap into it at any time, simply by opening up your mind to the possibility that all good exists for you. No one needs to have less in order for someone to have more. A lavish abundance already exists to meet your every desire. Ask for what you desire with the absolute certainty that it will be given to you. And it already has been!

Simply put, *The Art of Tithing* offers a systematic way to create true and lasting abundance in all areas of your life. This book is successfully used by people from all walks of life. It offers an easy way to dispel misconceptions and dissolve past discomfort about tithing and wealth.

Tithing is a way of saying "thank you" for the abundance that is manifesting or appearing in your life today and in the days to come. This pioneering book launched the contemporary prosperity movement and has created lasting change for readers in more than sixty-seven countries. By pondering the Discussion Questions and devoting yourself to doing the Activities, it can do the same for you.

Chapter One

Before Session 1:
- Read Chapter 1

During Session 1:
- Discuss your experience of tithing in your life
- Discuss your expectations of this program
- Discuss the questions at the end of this chapter

After Session 1:
- Begin tithing 1%
- Do one or more of the activities listed at the end of this chapter

In The Beginning

"A grateful mind is a great mind, which
eventually attracts to itself great things."
—PLATO

Every culture and every religion from the beginning of time understood that our abundance was a gift—freely given to us—and that we were somehow stewards of that abundance. Arabians, Babylonians, Buddhists, Chinese, Christians, Egyptians, Greeks, Hindus, American Indian, Jews, Muslims, Pagans, Persians, Phoenicians, Romans—every sect and every group—understood the spiritual basis of the ancient Divine Law of Prosperity.

This Divine Law is always active, even when we are unaware.

When I was a young girl, I used to spend my summers grandma-sitting my great-grandmother on her farm in northern Indiana. One of my favorite morning activities was harvesting the raspberries from the raspberry canes.

Each morning I'd go out with my little basket and I'd come back into the farmhouse kitchen with at least two pints of raspberries. One pint we would clean and put in the freezer; the other I'd sprinkle sugar on and eat for breakfast. I was amazed that every morning there were always at least two pints of raspberries waiting to be picked.

One summer it dawned on me that since there were two pints of raspberries to pick every day, I could save a lot of time and energy if I picked the raspberries once a week. That way, I could harvest all fourteen pints of raspberries at one time. Seemed brilliant to me!

A week passed and I ran to the raspberry patch and began harvesting my raspberries with great joy. When I finished, instead of the fourteen pints of raspberries I had anticipated, I still had only two pints. I couldn't understand what had happened. There should have been seven times as many raspberries, but there weren't.

Many years later, I understood what had happened that summer. As long as I embraced my abundant supply of raspberries every day, gave thanks for that abundance—through my willingness to pick my daily raspberries—my abundance continued. It was only when I stopped systematically giving thanks that the flow of abundance decreased.

Because I didn't show up to harvest my raspberries daily—because I didn't give thanks for the good I was already receiving with my thoughts, words and actions—the abundant flow of raspberries passed me by.

Some raspberries ripened and fell to the ground or were eaten by birds. Other raspberries simply didn't develop, since there was still an abundant supply on the canes that hadn't been harvested. Because I stopped giving thanks for the harvest of two pints of raspberries every day, the Universe didn't see any true sign that I would be happy with fourteen pints a week, either.

That was when I understood part of the Divine Law of Prosperity: Until you learn to be happy with what you have, you won't be happy with more.

The truth is, we have everything already. We have just forgotten that fact. We've stopped even noticing all the good in our lives. We're quick to jump on the bandwagon that says we "lack" something (whether it be peace of mind, material wealth, health, love, etc.). We won't become open and receptive to seeing any additional abundance in our life until we learn to notice and cheerfully embrace the abundance that surrounds us right now. We must see the good in *everything* that is showing up in our lives—whether it be in the form of money, ideas, people or opportunities. And we must give thanks for that abundance by giving back of our time, abilities, treasures and more.

The Art of Tithing is designed to help you tap into your innate abundance, using the core prosperity principle of tithing. Tithing is an ancient prosperity technique that reawakens your awareness that you are already fully immersed in the flow of Universal Energy and Abundance.

This reawakening is the true nature and power of tithing. Tithing isn't a financial transaction, although sometimes tithing involves giving and receiving financially. True tithing is so much deeper than money alone. The art of tithing helps you open up to greater good in all areas of your life. True tithing expands you. It helps you *be* more of who you truly are, *experience* more of what you truly desire and *do* more of what you love.

Tithing is about cultivating gratitude and thankfulness. It's about giving thanks for what already exists in your life, seen and unseen. By giving thanks with everything you are, everything you experience, everything you give and everything you receive, you expand your awareness and draw to you even greater visible good than you send out. *True tithing is a prayer of thanksgiving offered up in acknowledgment of our limitlessness.*

I will be the first to admit this book is not for everyone. In fact, this book may not be for most people. This book is for people who are strong enough, courageous enough and motivated enough to take the first step toward letting go of the illusion that the abundance in their lives comes from something *outside* of themselves. This book is designed to help you see the truth: our good doesn't come from our hard work, our jobs, our current or former spouse's income, our disability or unemployment checks, our parents' financial assistance or inheritance, the lottery, our cultural or economic status or any other force outside of us.

This book is for you if you're willing to set aside—even temporarily—any fears or objections that arise from the concept of God. Whatever name you give the expansive power from which our world sprang forth, there is one immutable truth you must be willing to embrace if you wish to gain the highest benefit from this material: *There is only one power and one presence in the Universe, a power that is only good, and from which everything in life unfolds, in Divine Order, for our highest good in a manner that completely matches our beliefs and thoughts.*

This Divine Love IN you, AS you, IS you.

This book is for you if you're willing to allow this truth to unfold in your life and to embrace this truth, no matter how it may appear to your ego. I encourage you to willingly stand in your fears and work through those fears to reach a point of true contentment, regardless of apparent circumstances.

This book is for you if you're ready to set aside skepticism and current beliefs about what you know about tithing to see the true meaning of the action behind the word. Your willingness to have an open mind makes it possible for you to fully embrace and harness the original intent of the tithing principle.

Embrace Your True Abundance

So how *do* we learn to recognize and embrace the abundance we experience? How do we learn to give thanks for everything that occurs so we can learn to recognize and receive all the good that is present and flowing in our lives? How do we get past the obstacles, explanations, excuses and fears that keep us from giving and receiving thanks—willingly, cheerfully and joyfully—in every moment of every day? I hope by the time you finish reading this book, you will know these answers for yourself.

We all have has our own issues around giving and receiving that need healing. The first step for many of us, when learning to give thanks, is learning to be open and accepting *receivers*. Fortunately, just as we've been conditioned *not* to receive, we can recondition ourselves to *willingly* receive everything that comes into our lives, even things we've designated as undesirable or disastrous.

For instance, I used to live in the boondocks about forty-five minutes from everything. Occasionally, I got stuck behind a slow-moving vehicle. I could choose to spend my time and energy trying to get around the slowpoke. I could try to race past him when we reached a town where the road became two lanes. I could fuss and fume and raise my blood pressure over the chance I would be late. Or I could assume that this condition, this slow-moving vehicle, had been placed in my path for a reason.

I could choose to receive this gift and give thanks for it, even though I might not be able to see *how* it might be for my highest good. The possibilities for good in our life are limited only by the limits of our imagination *and* the limits of our ability to receive.

Maybe if I'd been going faster I would have been involved in the accident whose aftermath I passed on the road a few minutes later. Or maybe I'd been running all week in such high gear, this gift from the Universe was allowing me to slow down and recenter. When we actively change the way we view events in our lives—when we can think of them not as *good* events or *bad* events, but as just *events*—we sync up with the universal energy that embodies limitless abundance.

When we stop trying to control the outcome of events, we demonstrate our willingness to let God reveal our abundance to us in the form it's supposed to take—even if that form is one we don't initially recognize as being for our highest good.

There is only one thing we can truly control: *our reactions to our thoughts.* If something disturbs you, stop adding it to your consciousness. If the news leaves you feeling angry or anxious, turn off the television or radio, cancel the newspaper, remove it from your Facebook feed. Want true happiness, peace of mind and abundance? Stop focusing on what's *not* working in your life and in the world. Start focusing on what *is* working.

We each have so much abundance in our lives, but most of us can't see it because it's not taking a form we recognize. We have our sights so set on abundance being a specific thing—like a raise or a bigger house or a particular wrong being righted in a specific way—we don't ever see our true abundance. Until we see it, embrace it and give thanks for it, we won't be in alignment with the infinite limitlessness contained in the universal energy that surrounds and infuses us.

Over time you will notice how all events in your life are (and have been) important steps toward your permanent prosperity. They are all part of your Universal or Divine Plan, *your* life's purpose. They are all unfolding in Divine Timing, according to Divine Law.

Here's a great example from my own life. In August of 2015, I was listening to a recorded talk my best friend Julie gave called "Giving Thanks." I suddenly remembered I hadn't renewed my car registration. I was out of state, so I dug out the paperwork and attempted to renew online, as I'd done before. This time, however, the system told me I had to renew in person, in Florida. My tags were set to expire at the end of August. Which was a week away. The rest of the week was full of classes to teach, important meetings, and a family wedding which I would be officiating in Colorado. My only open days were the next two days.

I sat still for a moment and was divinely guided to check on airfare. Great prices were to be found on next-day air travel. A rental car (with tax) would cost less than $20. As a bonus, I'd enjoy dinner and an overnight with Julie and her family—including my three-year-old godchild! Plus the Florida DMV allows you to "make appointments," assuring my car would be registered first thing that morning. I'd catch an early evening flight and be back in Colorado by mid-afternoon.

I flew home to Florida the next day, with plans to enjoy brunch and lunch out with various friends the following day. A different abundance awaited me. My brunch date turned into an all-day hangout with my bestie when her car wouldn't start again after dropping her daughter off at preschool. We spent much needed time together that would have been significantly shorter if I had stuck to my original plans.

As your perception toward abundance begins to shift, you will begin to unconsciously give thanks for the flow of every day, even when plans change. When you open your mind and heart to freely receive the limitless abundance available for you, you will find every area of your life improving. This is my greatest hope for you. It is why I wrote this book.

I am not joking when I tell you so much abundance swirls in and around each of our lives every moment— no one has yet built a container large enough to hold it all. Until the theory of gratitude is actively put it into practice through the art of tithing, you—like most people— will never experience even a fraction of the available abundance.

Are you ready to embrace illimitable abundance? Join me now in this most incredible adventure and put the art of tithing to work in your life, starting today!

Let's start with a little back story, shall we?

People from ancient cultures understood this knowledge: that their mind, body, soul—every possession and every idea they had—were instruments or channels of Divine abundance, which was synonymous with whatever name they gave to Universal Spirit. This is clear from

Egyptian hieroglyphics and Babylonian cuneiform tablets, as well as early Greek and Roman writings. Ancient Romans, for example, poured the first wine from each year's harvest onto the ground before taking a sip themselves, giving back the first portion to Mother Nature, whom they believed had graciously given it to them.

People everywhere have always searched for a way to consistently stay aware of their Oneness with the divinely inspired flow of abundance. To accomplish this, they followed two primary principles regarding their abundance.

First, they consistently gave forth the first portion of what they were given, to honor the Source of all their good.

Second, they gave this portion to wherever or whomever spiritually fed, helped or inspired them.

Before tithing was ever recorded in writing, it was handed down from generation to generation and understood as the *Divine Law of Prosperity.* Tithing was seen for what it was: an action to be taken in order to give thanks for the abundance that had already manifested, and to give thanks in advance for the greater good that was yet to appear, but which was already active and present in their lives.

Historically, tithing was considered an act of service and giving the tenth part, or the tithe, was an honorable action. The biblical story of Jacob illustrates the honor of tithing. When Jacob was a young man, he set off from home to find fame and fortune. One night during his journey, he awakened from a dream in which he saw himself being blessed by God. He was so grateful he immediately built a monument to God.

Then he made known the blessings he desired. He asked for financial prosperity, guidance, peace of mind and reconciliation with his family. He vowed in good faith to give God a tithe or one-tenth of everything that he was given, without even knowing whether or not God would provide these blessings. Jacob went on to become one of the Bible's early millionaires and within twenty years had realized these blessings.

What Exactly Is a Tithe?

Honor the Lord with thy substance,
and with the first fruits of all thine increase.
—THE BIBLE, BOOK OF PROVERBS (3:9)

Tithing is about saying "thank you," which always begins with putting some gratitude in our attitude. Giving thanks is about tithing not only with our money, but also with our thoughts, words, actions, time, efforts and possessions. What do these seven types of tithing look like?

1. Tithe from your resources: Give financially to everyone who feeds your spirit in some way. Give freely and joyfully with no expectation of getting anything in return and without judging who or where you give.

2. Tithe from your thoughts: Give thanks to everyone who comes into your life for the role they play in your life, whether or not it was a role you welcomed.

3. Tithe from your words: Speak words of love, gratitude and thanksgiving rather than criticism, condemnation and sarcasm.

4. Tithe from your actions: Act with integrity, honesty and courage rather than fear.

5. Tithe from your time: Volunteer; go out of your way to stop and help someone in need; put down your electronics or newspaper and truly listen when a child is speaking.

6. Tithe from your efforts: Approach everything you do with gratitude and joy, even if it's not what your ego desires to be doing at that moment.

7. Tithe from your possessions: Give to others, without expecting anything in return.

How and Why Tithing Works

People always ask me to explain why tithing works. You know the saying "you get more flies with honey than vinegar?" Have you ever noticed, when you smile at people, you are likely to get a smile in return? We are constantly sending either positive or negative energy into the universe. That energy is constantly multiplied and returned to us in kind. True tithing unleashes an energy of gratitude that works like a magnetic force, blessing and multiplying all you are, all you do and all you experience. If your magnetic force is negative, it will repel your good instead of attract it. Tithing helps you truly see that Divine Love IN you, AS you, IS you.

We tithe as a show of gratitude for what has already been revealed to us, and as a symbol of our gratitude for—and faith in—the fact that even greater good (which is already ours), is becoming visible. Tithing provides us with a proven, systematic way to multiply our good through a demonstration of our willingness to give back one-tenth of everything we've already received. Tithing demonstrates we are ready, willing and able to embrace an increased awareness of our limitless abundance. Tithing is a nonverbal way to say we are ready to perceive the omnipresent abundance that is manifest in our lives now—ever present.

The word *tithe* is based on the word *tenth*. It is a percentage. Ancient cultures believed the number ten was a powerful number of increase, symbolic of the whole. Everything begins and ends with ten. We count to ten, and then begin again, adding one to the next tenth. Computer languages are written with two binary numbers: 1 and 0. The number 1 reaffirms the Universal Truth that we are all One. We are all interconnected with God, the Universe, Spirit. *Divine Love IN us, AS us, IS us.* This connection is furthered by 0, which shows how there is no beginning and no ending, but only an eternal natural and spiritual cycle. Limitless flow, infinite.

When you give thanks for what God has provided you—by selflessly giving back one-tenth of what you've already received—you make yourself vividly aware of your Oneness with this cyclical flow. Your blessings are then multiplied tenfold, hundredfold, heck, billionfold. Once you recognize your true connection to this flow, the gratitude with which you give your tithe blesses others and yourself, which in turn increases the supply of visible abundance worldwide. We begin to recognize that there's always enough for everyone.

Jacob understood that tithing was an exercise in faith; a way of giving thanks for all that was in his life at that moment, as well as gratitude for the good that would appear to him, without any proof or evidence that this good *would* actually appear.

Tithing doesn't work just because you've given a tenth of your income to your church or temple, however. Too many people have approached tithing with the mindset that tithing is a duty or obligation. Or with an expectation of getting something in return.

Tithing is not about giving back to God out of duty, obedience or necessity, or giving in order to get something in return. Tithing is not about money, and it's not a religious injunction created by the Judeo-Christian religions. Tithing actually predates the Bible by centuries and has been practiced in various forms by all cultures.

Many cultures, wanting their people to know they were ever prospered, went so far as to make tithing a requirement. The giving of the tithe was written down in a specific legalistic form in the Talmud, the Jewish law, which also forms the first five books of today's Christian Bible. The various written laws created intense debate over what should be tithed, how much and to whom. Questions regarding the particulars of tithing laws still arise today among Talmudic scholars—and among Christian scholars who debate whether or not the laws of tithing pertain to members of their faith.

Somewhere along the way the intent of the law, the Spirit of the law, was lost. This is why Jesus stated that he came not to destroy the law, but to fulfill it. His purpose was to remind people of the Spirit of the law rather than the letter of the law. To remind people that God, Divine Love, is who we are—heart, soul and mind.

Jesus recognized the Spirit of the law was often being overlooked, and he sought to inspire people to embrace their personal connection to Spirit. To embrace the truth of our Oneness with God and, by extension, our Oneness with each other. That is why he provided a simplified version of all the commandments and laws:

1. Love God—the God of your Creation, the God of your Being, the God of your Understanding—with all your heart, soul and mind.
2. Love your neighbor as yourself.

Jesus sought to remind people that the tithe was not intended to be viewed as an obligation, duty, or act of obedience. The tithe was intended to be given willingly, cheerfully and joyfully as a love offering, a glad tiding. This is why Christian biblical texts refer to tithing as a *free-will offering*. Your tithe was to be given of your own free will, not out of any sense of duty or obligation. Right here and now, I hope to put to rest an enduring myth about tithing being an obligation. The truth is, you do not have an *obligation* to tithe—you have an *opportunity* to tithe.

Story after story abounds of those who gave obligatory tithes but who were not blessed, because their tithe was given routinely, with no thought toward gratitude or thanksgiving. Tithing became a household chore, and people gave of the first and the best of all they had routinely. They still brought their tithes to the temples, had great feasts and gave their tithes to the priests to be used by them to help feed others—spiritually and literally. But more and more, the tithe was seen as just another obligation, not as an opportunity to give thanks.

Whether you call it a glad offering, a free-will offering, a heave offering, a love offering, or any other name, a true tithe is always extended as an offering of *gratitude*. When you begin to give freely and release your need to control the outcome of *how* your good shows up in your life, you make it possible for that good to appear. Let me illustrate this with a quick story (you will find this book peppered with stories like this one):

A songwriter found herself in the red financially. Several clients owed her money. Rather than spend her time and energy worrying about what she didn't have, she affirmed *"The Universe will take care of me. It always does. I'm sick of worrying."*

She was guided to go to her post office box, where she discovered a check from a musician to whom she had gifted one of her songs to record. She had given her song freely—without asking for any royalty—because she knew the musician would create a beautiful rendition.

Her good was multiplied and returned to her in an unexpected way.

This woman discovered that tithing takes many forms, but has one common theme: A tithe is something you give to another without any expectation of anything in return.

In the case of tithes, size doesn't matter; intent does.

Session 1 Questions for Discussion

1. How have you been conditioned to receive or to *not* receive in the past? What were you taught about receiving?

2. When people attempt to give you things, what assumptions are you making about them when you accept or turn down their gifts? What assumptions are you making in your life?

3. What are you willing to stop adding to your consciousness? (Examples might be the news, gossip, negative self-talk.)

4. What other things would you like to stop adding to your consciousness, that you don't see *how* you can do so? Would you be willing to let go of these things as well if you knew how?

5. Since our reaction to our thoughts is the only thing we can truly control, which of your current reactions are you willing to start controlling?

6. What have you noticed is different about your perspective on prosperity and abundance since you began reading *The Art of Tithing*?

Session 1 Activities (do one or more after Session 1)

1. Make a list of all major events from your life, no matter whether you originally thought they were good events or bad events. Write down the good that *may* have resulted from these events. Write down all the ways you can think of that each event helped you be who you are, where you are today. Write down how each event has helped make you a better person. Write down how each event helped you be more authentically you.

   For example, if the author of this book hadn't gone bankrupt, she wouldn't have written *Bounce Back From Bankruptcy*, she wouldn't have helped people have healthier relationships with money. She would have never written *this* book. And you wouldn't be reading it right now.

   Examples from your own life could be something like, "If I hadn't divorced/been widowed/ended my relationship with a previous love interest, I wouldn't have the freedom or the new relationship I have today." Or, "If I hadn't been fired, I wouldn't have this great new job, this particular new friend I met while looking for work, or had the courage to start my own company . . ."

You get the idea.

2. Use the *Prosperity Tracker* (located at the back of this book) to list all prosperity you receive in each column. (For your convenience, you can download a full size copy of the *Prosperity Tracker* at https:// paulalangguthryan.com/free)

Now that you've completed Session 1, begin tithing 1%

Chapter Two

Before Session 2:

· Read Chapter 2

During Session 2:

· Discuss your experience doing
the activities after Session 1

· Discuss the questions at the end of this chapter

After Session 2:

· Begin tithing 2%

· Do one or more of the activities listed
at the end of this chapter

Misconceptions About Tithing

A mind once stretched by a new idea can never go back to its original dimensions.

—Oliver Wendell Holmes

In 1940, a man named Perry Hayden proved that every harvest is an increase or multiplication of the seeds we plant. Farmers can only plant a new crop if they set aside seed or money from the current crop to purchase the future seed. We can only do the same in our lives. Like the Biblical story of Jacob, we too can plant our seeds and reap our harvest in all areas of our lives.

People are often confused about tithing, based on misconceptions they grew up believing. Hopefully, this chapter will help clear up some of that confusion. Like Oliver Wendell Holmes said, a mind once stretched by a new idea can never go back to its original dimensions. So, let's start by looking at what tithing is *not*.

Tithing is not about giving money to spiritual leaders, although tithes should always be given to those who provide you with spiritual help, or feed your spirit with inspiration and joy. This could be your local church, temple, mosque or synagogue, an inspirational writer, speaker or musician, or elsewhere.

Tithing is not about bribing some God or Universal Energy *out there*, in order to get more abundance. Tithing is not about keeping score of the gifts we gain in return. The idea that it is better to give than to receive has merit, but presents a peculiar paradox. It is both *giving* and *receiving* that create a greater awareness of the abundant good existing in all areas of our lives. More about this later.

Many people think of tithing as a way to give in order to get something in return. Obedience. Duty. A requirement. A way to avoid disappointing God. Tithing is none of these things.

Tithing is like breathing. You can hold your breath anytime you want. You can hold your breath until you turn blue and pass out. Then the natural rhythm of breathing will take over unconsciously. You'll begin giving and receiving air—in and out—whether you want to or not.

Becoming aware of how you unconsciously breathe or hold your breath in times of stress can help you create greater health in your life. The same is true with tithing. Becoming aware of the ways you unconsciously tithe, or withhold your tithe, will help you create greater abundance in your life.

You can withhold your tithe anytime you want, but your tithe will be paid somewhere, somehow. The natural law of giving and receiving demands it, because there is a Spiritual or Cosmic cause to every effect. You can consciously give thanks to the places that *feed* your spirit, or you can unconsciously give to the places that *deplete* your spirit. When you don't tithe to your spiritual Source, you wind up tithing elsewhere.

A woman tithed and saved $417 on auto parts. Another woman tithed and received a lower mortgage rate than the one she had locked into. A man tithed and he lost weight, thereby alleviating health problems.

A woman withheld her tithe and her purse was stolen. A man decided to withhold his tithe after years of tithing and building a prosperous business. The following year his business fell into financial ruin. Another woman tithed regularly to a place that no longer fed her spirit, and was unable to break free from persistent financial difficulties.

Tithing offers you an incredible opportunity to take control of your future by releasing—giving forth—a portion of what you've been given, with gratitude and joy.

This is the paradox of tithing. The only way to control your future abundance is to relinquish control of a portion of your current abundance. The choice is up to you. You can choose whether you want to be aware and conscious of the circulation in your life or not. You can choose to actively make things happen in your life or passively allow them to happen. Remember: You have no *obligation* to tithe; only an *opportunity*. What you do with that opportunity is up to you.

The Truth About Tithing

The greater the truth to be expressed, the more simply can it (and should it) be clothed.

—H. Emilie Cady

In its truest form, tithing is simply a way of saying *thank you* for the good appearing in your life today and in the days to come. Walter Russell said, "All knowledge can be obtained from the Universal Source of All Knowledge by becoming One with that Source."

Tithing is an acknowledgment that we *are* One with that Source. Tithing is a way of giving thanks for everything that has ever appeared in your life. It's also a way of giving thanks in advance for the greater good that you are about to perceive. Yes, *perceive.*

Tithing is about giving thanks for the past, present and future all at the same time. Tithing plops you squarely down in the flow of abundance. The practice of tithing involves giving back a percentage—one-tenth or 10%—of what you've been given, to places that feed your soul spiritually.

I know 10% can seem like a huge amount, especially when our egos are bent on convincing us that we don't have *enough*—which is why this is a *gradual* tithing program. You start out tithing 1%. Then, each session—weekly or monthly—you increase your tithes by 1% until you easily and effortlessly find yourself giving 10% by the end of the book.

The *Divine Law of Prosperity*, which includes the principle of tithing, is a universal, immutable, eternal Truth. This law is governed by order and harmony and is a law in the same way the Law of Gravity is a law. The *Divine Law of Prosperity* follows all the rules of physics:

1. An object in motion tends to stay in motion unless it is acted upon by an equal, opposite force.
2. An object at rest tends to stay at rest unless it is acted upon by an outside force greater than itself.

Likewise, the awareness of your abundance continues to grow unless it is stopped by a force that is equal to and opposite itself. Your awareness grows in direct proportion to your giving and gratitude. The more gratefully you give and receive, the more visible your good becomes. This universal truth is timeless, just like gravity.

Gravity did not begin at the point when Isaac Newton got bonked on the head with an apple or at the point when he calculated and wrote down the equations that make up the Law of Gravity. Nor did tithing begin when it was first recorded in the Bible or when it was set down as a law in the Mosaic Covenant or whenever you first learned about tithing. The prospering power of tithing, like the grounding force of gravity, has existed from time immemorial.

The effects of tithing, like the effects of gravity, do not occur because we make it so or because we recognize its existence. Gravity does not cease to exist when you enter an anti-gravity chamber or sail off in a rocket into outer space.

In these instances, you have merely stopped the Law of Gravity from having any *influence* in your life at that moment. The pull of gravity still exists and is still at work in your life, whether you are physically present in a gravitational field or not. The prospering power of tithing still exists and is still at work whether or not you have physically placed yourself in the flow of abundance. The only thing that changes—if you decide not to tithe—is the strength of the law's effect on your life.

The Law of Geometry is another example of a universal law in action. What do you know about triangles? The sum of the angles of any triangle will always equal two right angles, or 180 degrees. You can draw any triangle, and before you put pen to paper, I can tell you with *absolute certainty* that the sum of all three angles will equal 180 degrees. Get out your paper and pen and protractor and I'll wait while you draw a gazillion triangles, if—like me—you need to prove this theorem for yourself.

Everything that is freely given with thanks will be multiplied and returned to you in expected and unexpected ways.

—THE DIVINE LAW OF PROSPERITY

You may have already known that the sum of the angles of a triangle always equals 180 degrees, or you may have just learned this fact from me. You knowing it or not knowing it does not make it any more or less true. This law was true even before anyone recognized it. It is true today. It will be true forever because it is based on an immutable or unchangeable law. You see where I'm going with this?

These laws are everlasting, like sunshine. The sun is *always* shining. The rotation of the earth does not cause the sun to stop shining. The passage of a cloud in front of the sun does not stop it from shining. Even if we are in some dark, windowless basement or prison cell, far removed from any source of light, the sun does not stop shining. We may gain no comfort or joy from the sunshine in these instances—the sun may not be shining on *us*—but the sun itself never stops shining.

So it is with our blessings, when we remove ourselves from the Universal flow or source of those blessings—which is already within us. Cease giving thanks for what you've received—for what is currently showing up in your life and for all that is ahead of you—and you remove yourself from the influence of the *Divine Law of Prosperity.* You remove yourself from the benefits of tithing.

The *Divine Law of Prosperity* still exists, and our blessings are still being poured out, but we are no longer being the great big blessing that tithing turns us into. We're not present to giving or receiving blessings.

Only two things can stand in the way of experiencing the unlimited supply the Universe has for us. The first is our own ignorance or lack of knowledge about the true, divine model of supply and demand. The second is our willfulness.

We may know on some level that tithing works. Unless we become willing to put the principles to work in our lives, however, we won't experience the full force of the abundant flow of prosperity. Want to test the theory of tithing for yourself? Want to see how you can put the prospering power of tithing to work in your life?

First, you must learn how to give without attachment. Second, you have to learn how to give in gratitude and with thankfulness. Finally, you have to learn how to give thanks for what you already have in all areas of your life—even when what you have doesn't look anything like what your ego would have chosen for you.

When you give thanks for every bit of Divine Love that is swirling around in your world, the Universe responds by opening up your vision so you can actually perceive the ever present good in your life. You will be amazed as you begin to notice and recognize all the forms of rich ideas, gifts and blessings that are ever present in all areas of your life. Remember: *Divine Love IN you, acting AS you, IS you.*

We have to learn how to let go of our attachment to the outcome of events in our lives. The mantra of "I want what I want when I want it" needs to be replaced by a willingness to let things unfold in Divine Order. Our tiny view and perception of the abundance in our lives is beyond microscopic. Let go of your *expectations* of "how" something should appear in your life. When you do, you make room for the *expectancy* that everything appearing in your life *is* for your highest good, even if you don't see *how* in the present moment. If what appears *isn't* for your highest good, it *wouldn't* be showing up!

The Natural Benefits of Tithing

God multiplies blessings back to us and brings us out of the
land of just enough and into the land of abundance.

—REV. BOB YANDIAN

Ready to meet Perry Hayden? In 1940, Perry planted one cubic inch of wheat, in a plot four feet by eight feet (just to give you some perspective, it takes 2,150 cubic inches to make a bushel). From that first planting, he harvested 50 cubic inches of wheat. He tithed ten percent to a local Quaker community and planted the remaining 45 cubic inches of wheat the next spring. By the third year, the amount of land required to plant the increase had grown from the original 48 square foot plot to one acre. By the fifth year, the amount of land required to plant the increase had grown to 230 acres and yielded 5,555 bushels of wheat.

Once you make a commitment to tithe the first fruits of your labor—the first ten percent of all that you have, are and receive, to your Spiritual Source—like Jacob and Perry, you will discover the benefits of tithing.

Abundance doesn't come merely as a cash windfall. When you open your perception to the full flow of the *Divine Law of Prosperity* by actively tithing with gratitude, you will receive creative and inspired ideas, gifts of all kinds, wisdom and guidance, improved relationships, increased health, the best customers, clients, contracts, opportunities, deals—and so much more. In all ways, your prosperity becomes fully visible to you.

You will also experience more joy, vitality, freedom and peace of mind. Tithing helps you be in the right place at the right time; it puts you in alignment with your highest good and lifts you above ego thoughts that judge situations as good or bad.

I might not have believed all these benefits if not for an admitted packrat who wrote to tell me what happened when he began tithing of his possessions. One month, he tithed possessions in addition to his monetary tithe, equal in value to 65% of his income; the next month, 67%. Each month he found he was able to pay off over $1,500 worth of debts. He had not been able to pay so much on his debt in many months. He also lost weight, received a rent reduction, and unexpected cash totaling $700. And he credits tithing as the reason he avoided losing $45,000.

As he related to me, he had put a $105,000 bid on a house he wanted to buy. But the deal would not go through. One delay after another occurred. Eventually, he withdrew his offer. He later discovered the house had major foundation problems and wasn't worth more than $60,000. Had the sale gone through, he would have owned a house worth $45,000 *less* than what he had paid.

Tithing may not necessarily bring you *more* money. It may just provide you with a more efficient and effective distribution system for the money you already have, which may be what you truly need.

When famine swept Ethiopia in the 1980's, a massive global relief effort was undertaken and more than five hundred tons of grain were shipped to Ethiopia.

Despite these efforts, very few hungry people were fed and the grain rotted in warehouses in the port cities. Ethiopia didn't need more food. They needed more trucks and better roads. The country had enough food. It merely needed a better *distribution* system, so the food they had could be circulated to everyone in the country.

You already have everything. You simply do not realize it. You already have enough money—but you may not have the best system in place to allow you to use your money for the purpose you desire.

Everything we desire doesn't always show up in the form in which we desire it, especially when we hire our ego to chauffeur our thoughts around. When we fire ego, we more clearly see that Divine Love IN us, acting AS us, IS us. That Divine Love, which I call God, often gives us the tools that we require to succeed and then guides us to discover how to use these tools in ways that benefit all, not just ourselves.

This is exactly what Mary Hart, the long-running host of the *Entertainment Tonight* show, proved in her own life.

In 1979, she left journalism behind. She drove to Los Angeles with $10,000 in the bank and dreams of acting stardom. She wanted to have her own show to be reported on; she didn't want to report on the acting business. When offered the opportunity to host *Entertainment Tonight*, however, she accepted the opportunity.

She lived in Westwood and jogged through the swank neighborhoods of Holmby Hills and Beverly Hills, consciously saying to herself every day, "Someday I will be successful enough to live in this neighborhood." *How* it happened wasn't of concern to her; she simply visualized herself in that upper class community. She and her family eventually lived in one of those neighborhoods for many years.

What Mary Hart ultimately learned was that she was in the best place she could have been in. She once said, "I knew this job was good and I knew it was fun, being thrust into the middle of all these situations that

I dreamed about. But just in a different way than I'd dreamed about."

When you practice the art of tithing, you will receive six incredible benefits:

1. Increased wisdom and good judgment
2. Increased health
3. Increased wealth and a greater ability to meet expenses and reduce debt (often through the reduction of those expenses)
4. Increased fulfillment in relationships
5. Increased spiritual understanding
6. A willingness to let go of your expectations of what you believe you desire—so you can become open and receptive to receiving what will benefit you the most.

When you begin realizing these benefits, you will be able to give even greater good, above and beyond the first ten percent. Many other industrious and prosperous business leaders practiced tithing, including the Colgate, Kraft, Templeton and Heinz families. William Colgate learned about tithing from an old riverboat captain. Colgate ultimately tithed 50% of his annual income and his bookkeeping records were marked "Account With the Lord."

When people chastised John D. Rockefeller for having so much money, he was not dismayed or ashamed of his wealth. He simply stated one true fact to those who criticized him. He told them, "God gave me my money." Rockefeller started tithing in 1855. His income that year was $95 and he tithed $9.50 to his local church. Between 1855 and 1934, he gave away over $531 million, tithing far more than 10% of what he had been given.

In fact, some people who tithe eventually discover they can effortlessly give away 90% of their income and live comfortably on the remaining 10%. Rockefeller experienced this joy, as did R. G. LeTourneau (the man who invented the heavy equipment that later became the foundation of the Caterpillar company) and Rev. Stretton Smith (creator of the *4T Prosperity Program*).

What did they know that we don't know? Their families taught them how to be good stewards of the abundance they had received. They were taught—just as Biblical stories show that Abraham taught his son Isaac and Isaac taught his son Jacob—to give thanks for what they had been given, by giving back. You may have been taught tithing. You may have been taught the rightful purpose of tithing or that tithing was an obligation or a duty, if that is what your family believed.

Either way, having the knowledge about tithing is not what prospers you, any more than having the knowledge that the angles of a triangle always equal 180 degrees helps you be a better builder. You have to put your knowledge into action. These successful people learned the fundamentals of how to tithe from their families, but it wasn't until they seized the opportunity to *practice* the art of tithing that they were prospered in all areas of their lives.

Acts of impersonal, selfless giving prosper us. Tithes given willingly, cheerfully and joyfully are the tithes that count. These are the true tithes, no matter how large or small.

In a story found in the biblical book of Mark (12:41–44), Jesus watches as people give their tithes to the temple and he comments on a woman who *willingly* gave her last two copper coins to the temple, saying, "I tell you the truth, this poor widow has put more into the treasury than all the others. They all gave out of their wealth; but she, out of her poverty, put in everything—all that she had to live on."

The joy with which we give is what empowers a tithe. Whatever you give, give it with praise and thanksgiving, not out of resignation, desperation or with annoyance. When you give your tithe you must learn to give it—as you should with any gift—without attachment.

Here's a perfect example. A man I know—who often fed the spirit of his fellow churchgoers—was preparing to begin his ministerial studies. Many members of his church tithed to him for his lodging, transportation and tuition. When his circumstances changed and he was unable to attend as planned, he tithed what he had been given to someone who fed *his* spirit, whom he knew also wanted to enter the ministry.

This caused concern among the people who had tithed to him. Some people who had given to him were aghast that their gift had not been used as they had *expected*.

Seeing their turmoil, I asked them, "Was the money a gift or a loan?" "A gift," they replied. I then asked, "When you give a gift, who does it then belong to?" "The person you gave it to," they replied. "Then it belongs to him, and what *he* does with it is none of *your* business."

When you judge yourself or others and find a shortfall of some sort, stop and acknowledge your judgment. If you find yourself judging a financial situation or choice someone is making, especially with a gift or tithe you gave them, it is usually because you are being reminded of an event in your life where *you* felt judged by someone. Ask yourself: Who in my life did I perceive as having judged what I did with *their* money?

The following *Dollar a Day Exercise* will help you release resentments and attachments to money you give. Take a dollar (or your currency of choice) every day, and give it away to the third person you meet that day. Tell them you wanted them to have this gift. Pay attention to both *their* reaction and *your* reaction. Write down everything that comes into your head about what you think they will do with the money and how you feel about it. Then ask yourself *why* you believe it matters what *they* do with *their* money? How does what they do with *their* money relate to you?

Remember the last time you gave a gift or did something nice for someone and didn't receive so much as a "thank you" in return? That person's perceived lack of gratitude made you think twice about going out of your way to give them more, didn't it?

Have you ever bought a toy for a child? What usually happens? You give the child the gift and within ten minutes the toy is in pieces. Or you give the gift and never receive a "thank you," much less a thank-you note. What thoughts run through your head at these times?

"Why did I spend my money on that?" "That's the last time I'm going to waste my money like that." These are the thoughts of lack that enter our heads whenever we give with an attachment. We have the misconception that somehow we lost money when we bought the gift, or that we lost respect or honor, because we believe our gift wasn't properly appreciated or valued—that *we* weren't properly appreciated or valued.

Our attachments and expectations make us susceptible to the belief that somehow we can lose something in our lives. The Law of Energy has proven otherwise. Everything in the universe is made up of energy. And energy can be neither lost nor destroyed—it can only be converted.

The Power of Covenants

Covenants are a powerful tool for intentionally releasing expectations and attachments. A covenant is a solemn contract between you and your spiritual source.

These documents can take the form of a vow, a dedication, or a listing of your true heart's desires. They are intensely personal and exceedingly powerful. Here are four examples of covenants that are vastly different in *form* and yet quite similar in *substance*.

The first covenant is the biblical Jacob's vows as found in *Genesis*. The second is a dedication and covenant Charles and Myrtle Fillmore wrote when they created the long-standing prayer ministry known today as Silent Unity. I have a framed copy of this dedication and covenant hanging in my office.

The third covenant is a solemn acceptance of the desires of the heart created by my dear friends and spiritual parents, Kaye and Jervais Phillips. The final covenant is the dedication and covenant my beloved and I wrote when we created our first home together; it still hangs on our refrigerator today.

Notice the similarities and differences in each covenant and how they are equally powerful in their own way. Your intent, rather than the specific language you use, is most important in the process of creating your own covenant.

Sample Covenants

Covenant of Jacob from the Bible: And Jacob vowed a vow, saying, If God will be with me, and will keep me in this way that I go, and will give me bread to eat, and raiment to put on, so that I come again to my father's house in peace; then shall the Lord be my God: And this stone, which I have set for a pillar, shall be God's house: and of all that thou shalt give me I will surely give the tenth unto thee. (*Genesis, 28:20-22*)

Charles and Myrtle Fillmore Dedication and Covenant: We, Charles Fillmore and Myrtle Fillmore, husband and wife, hereby dedicate ourselves, our time, our money, all we have and all we expect to have, to the Spirit of Truth, and through it, to the Society of Silent Unity.

It being understood and agreed that the Said Spirit of Truth shall render unto us an equivalent for this dedication, in peace of mind, health of body, wisdom, understanding, love, life and an abundant supply of all things necessary to meet every want without our making any of these things the object of our existence.

In the presence of the Conscious Mind of Christ Jesus, this 7th day of December AD 1892

Kaye and Jervais Phillips Desires of the Heart: These are our desires:

An expanding awareness of our oneness with God. A relationship with each other that is continually fascinating, expanding, joyful and blissful. Relationships with our family and friends that are peaceful, harmonious, healthy, enjoyable and prosperous for us all. Experiences in which we are passionately involved that are motivated by love and joy and produce good and prosperity for us and those around us. An expanding awareness and manifestation of youthful bodies and alert minds that continually demonstrate energy, health and wholeness. An expanding awareness and use of God's rich abundance and endless supply to tithe, use and give with joy. A home that is beautiful, functional, reliable, comfortable and debt free. Frequent periods of rest, relaxation and enjoyment to be aware of and reflect on Divine Ideas.

We are thankful for the fulfillment of these desires now.

Haynes Family Dedication and Covenant: We do hereby declare that this house is a sanctuary. We dedicate it, ourselves, and all our resources, to creating a healing space in service of God.

Everyone is welcome.

Everyone is safe.

Everyone is Loved.

This home shall be known as the Divine Center of Light.

Session 2 Questions for Discussion

1. What good did you find in an event this past week that you would have normally judged as a bad event in the past?
2. What do you make room for when you let go of your expectations? How does this feel different than having an expectation?
3. What two primary principles of tithing can you practice to consistently stay in touch with your divinely inspired flow of good?
4. What are the seven ways you can tithe or give thanks?
5. What are some of the common misconceptions about tithing and which ones have you held in the

past? How has your thinking about tithing evolved since you started this program?

6. How do you unconsciously tithe, even when you withhold your tithe? Name a few of the ways your tithe has been "unconsciously" paid in the past. (Things taken from you, deals falling through, items lost, roadblocks and obstacles, items needing repair, etc.)

Session 2 Activities (do one or more after Session 2)

1. What three things can you begin to do each day, between now and Session 3, to become more present to receiving your blessings? Make a covenant with God (or whatever word you call that Divine Love IN you, AS you, that IS you), outlining one specific thing you can be more conscious of in each of these three areas:

   a. Giving without attachment.

   b. Giving in gratitude and with thankfulness for what you've already received.

   c. Giving thanks for something that appears in your life when it doesn't look anything like what you would have chosen.

2. Read aloud the covenants included in this chapter. Quietly contemplate your own covenant. Write down all the blessings you desire, like Jacob, Charles and Myrtle, Kaye and Jervais and Sandy and me.

3. Set an intention of something you desire to perceive in your life. Make *what* you want as specific as you can, without specifying *how* it must come to you. Begin your intention with "I see myself with the right and perfect_____. (Fill in the blank with something tangible or intangible—car, home, job, relationship, peace of mind, level of joy, health, etc.).

4. Share intentions with your study group. Read each person's intention to yourself or aloud, starting the covenant with "I see you. . . ." Finish by reading your own intention. "I see myself. . . ." Picture each person's true desires becoming visible in their lives. *Know* that what is in their life (and in your life) right now is the right and perfect manifestation for where each of you are at in your consciousness. See each person's consciousness expanding to a point of readiness to receive the next right and perfect step in their manifestation.

5. Use a fresh *Prosperity Tracker* to track the good that comes to you this week.

Now that you've completed Session 2, begin tithing 2%

Chapter Three

Before Session 3:

• Read Chapter 3

During Session 3:

• Discuss your experience doing
the activities from Session 2

• Discuss the questions at the end of this chapter

After Session 3:

• Begin tithing 3%

• Do one or more of the activities listed
at the end of this chapter

Tap Into Spiritual Flow

Jehovah-jireh: The mighty One whose presence and power provides, regardless of any opposing circumstances.

—CHARLES FILLMORE

You can tap into the spiritual flow in your life in two ways: as abundance flows into your life and as it flows out.

As I said earlier, in its most literal sense, tithing is defined as giving away a tenth, usually ten percent of your income. In a broader sense, however, the art of tithing involves sharing a tenth of your time, abilities and treasures—including your income—with people or organizations that feed your soul, as a way of giving thanks for the good that appears in your life and that is surrounding you. Wherever you receive spiritual inspiration, joy and help is where you should tithe.

Always tithe to places that spiritually feed you. Your local spiritual home and leaders are the best starting point, if that is where you receive your spiritual "aha moments."

Some other places to tithe include musicians, children, waitresses, speakers, writers, sometimes friends or family members, spiritual organizations, ministers, producers of television shows and movies, first responders, podcast hosts, teachers—anyone who provides inspiration and uplifts your spirit. Doing so places you directly in the flow of Universal Energy and Abundance and helps you experience greater good than what you send out.

A tenth is described as "a small percentage." Yet ten percent can seem like a lot of money, can't it? When I first starting tithing, there were days where the bills were coming in and a due date was looming and the checkbook balance looked a little slim when I thought, *I don't know if I can afford to tithe this week.* When I examined my fear, I discovered I had a false belief that my tithe was coming from *my* money, and that there was a limit to how much money I would, or could, have.

You may struggle with the concept of tithing because you think you are giving away 10% of what is *yours* instead of giving thanks for everything (100%) you have been given, by passing along 10% as seed money for the future. This may be because you have an attachment to the 10%. True freedom comes from letting go of our attachments.

I had the good fortune, years ago, to spend time with a well-to-do woman whose children attended the inner city school where she taught. She often opened her home readily to her children's less well-off schoolmates even when she wasn't home. Her friends and co-workers expressed dismay. Any time they had done the same, items they owned went missing. This woman believed firmly that everything in her home was merely a possession and that if a child truly thought he or she needed it more, they would take it, regardless of whether she was there to stand guard. She knew she was the steward, not the owner, of these possessions. She trusted God—not the schoolchildren—to do what was right and fair with these items. She released her attachment to these items. As a result, nothing was ever taken from her home.

Was this difference due to her non-attachment? A good question. Oddly enough, the woman was *very* attached to her solitude at home. All she wanted was for them to leave her alone, unbothered, when they came over to play. No matter how many times she reminded them, they would always find a way to interrupt her.

I share this powerful example to show you the truth about attachments. An attachment is simply an outward manifestation of our fears. When you look at your life through your fears, the view is similar to what you see when you look through a kaleidoscope. Everything in your life appears fractured. When you dismantle the kaleidoscope, the whole picture clearly appears and you can see the fractured illusion is caused by nothing more than three mirrors and a few bits of broken glass.

Scientists have proven that everything, everywhere, is made up of the same subatomic particles. There is nothing that is not part of this invisible substance. Everything and everyone is connected and part of the whole of the Universe.

What name do you give this connected substance? God, Universal Energy, Spirit, Infinite Intelligence, Divine Love?

Call this substance Divine Love and you will see that Divine Love is within everything—within every visible form we see, and in all the things we cannot see. There is nothing that is not made up of Divine Love. Every idea we have was inspired, meaning it was *in Spirit* before it was made manifest. Everything we possess is part of and on loan from Universal Energy, because everything is created from this inspirational energy. Divine Love IN you, AS you, IS you.

Until you come to this awareness of the wholeness of the Universe—that you are one with, and the steward of, the abundance in your life—you will be afraid to give your full tithe. As you work to overcome this fear and release your attachment, start the habit of giving a set percentage regularly (even 1%) until you can cheerfully, willingly and joyfully give a full 10% tithe—or more! The *only* time you should tithe is when you can do so cheerfully, willingly and joyfully.

A woman came to me upon hearing that I would soon be speaking at her church. She said every week she thinks about tithing. Every week she gets out her checkbook and says, "Okay, this will be the week I will tithe." But every week a fear steps in her way, and she freezes; unable to tithe.

So she gives what she can give willingly, cheerfully and joyfully that day. And you know what? Because of her willingness, and her attitude around her "tithing adventures," she will likely receive a greater blessing for her *partial* tithe than the person who resentfully or fearfully writes a check for a full 10%. The person who views the tithe as an obligation, duty, or as a way to *get* something will prosper less than one who gives what he feels capable of giving, but gives it lovingly, cheerfully and willingly.

The overwhelming prosperity you will experience when you willingly and cheerfully give a portion of your tithe is but a fraction of what is available to you once you can move beyond fear and begin tithing a full 10%. The truth is, you already have everything. Our fears simply keep this abundant supply from being known to us. Once you get out of your own way and allow God to take the reins, abundance will come galloping into view in your life.

Meet Your Every Need

Prosperity depends less on our financial situation
than on the extent to which our needs are being met.
—SHAKTI GAWAIN

Whatever percentage you give away to places that feed your spirit, always write your tithe check first. Do this for 30 days and you will soon see that the 90% you have left over after tithing throughout the month often goes as far, or farther, than the original 100%. Even if your income doesn't increase visibly, you'll find you can still do as much or more with the remaining 90%. That is because tithing connects you to God's flow of Universal Energy and Abundance.

Imagine, if you will, a space heater. The space heater has a power cord which is plugged into a socket. The space heater is connected to the flow of energy. However, the space heater can't access the flow of energy simply by being plugged in. Something has to happen to open the pathway to the energy. You need to flip the switch. Like the space heater, you're always connected to Universal Abundance. Flashes of inspiration come when we are plugged into the Universe, but we need to flip the switch in order to fully access this flow of abundance and inspiration. That's what tithing does. Tithing is the switch.

What happens when you flip on the space heater's switch? Once the heater accesses the flow of energy, you begin to experience an increase in heat flowing into the room. At the same time, you also have a decrease of cold in the room. It's a two-fold experience. Like the space heater, tithing places you firmly in the flow of abundance where you have an *increase* in your awareness of the good you have available to you, and a *decrease* in expenses that occur.

A woman began tithing and noticed that, while no windfall of cash had dropped in her lap, her expenses seemed to be going down. She closed on a house where she had locked in a certain interest rate. To her surprise, the rate on the mortgage was *lower*, resulting in lower monthly payments. In addition, her closing costs were $500 less and her car insurance dropped $20 a month. When she added up the savings, they totaled far more than she had tithed to date.

This is how the 90% left after tithing goes farther than the original 100%—even with no increase in your income. The Universal Energy automatically meets your every need in response to your act of gratitude.

A friend and I once ordered a pizza. When we went to pick up the pizza, we were asked to wait a few minutes, so we joyfully wandered outside. When we came back, the pizza man said, "Ladies, your pizza will be on the house. We had to remake it." With no effort on our part, we received the gift of a free dinner with a hearty "thank you."

If you are eager to give, your gift is accepted by the Universe on the basis of what you *have* to give, not on what you *don't have*. In other words, give what you can cheerfully give, but give in a systematic manner.

When you give systematically to the Universe, the Universe will see even more clearly that you are ready to reap a larger harvest. Remember those raspberries from Chapter 1? Some years, I harvested raspberries for weeks after the growing season should have ended, simply because I got up every morning and harvested the raspberries. I took the action and the results followed.

Here's an example of how taking action led to huge results for a church who reached out to me for guidance in changing their consciousness.

A church had stopped tithing or giving money to other organizations. Overall income had fallen off. The church had used up its savings to make ends meet and had fallen into debt.

I immediately encouraged the Trustees to tithe, but they were fearful. How could the church make ends meet with the 90% left over after tithing when they were unable to make ends meet with 100% of the church's current income? The Treasurer, an accountant by trade, was especially skeptical. I asked the Trustees to test the principle of tithing in a way that was not fearful to them. Eventually, after much discussion amongst themselves, they agreed to step out in faith and tithe 3% of the income from *just* the Sunday services.

Over the next six months, the church tithed $371. Amazing things happened during that time. An internationally acclaimed speaker who normally charged $3,500 to speak called and asked if he could speak for free. Moved by his speaking, someone put a $1,600 check in the offering basket—which was more than the amount usually collected at a Sunday service. Within two years, the church was tithing a full 10% of its income from all sources, had paid off all outstanding debts and had over $25,000 in savings.

This is just one example of what happens when you start embracing your abundance by systematically giving thanks for your existing good. The person who plants few seeds will have a small crop; the one who plants many seeds will have a large crop. Give as you have decided, not with regret or out of a sense of duty. God is able to give you more than you need, so that you will always have all you need for yourself and more than enough for every good cause. Give generously and your kindness will last forever.

Giving generously brings us back to the idea of stewardship. When we release our attachment to the idea that the abundance in our lives comes from us and from our actions, then we will truly prosper. We *are* illimitable. It's our natural state of being. Giving with gratitude simply opens our eyes to see this truth from a right perspective.

If someone handed you $1,000 with no strings attached, would you be willing to give them $100 back, if you had no obligation ever to repay the remaining $900? That's exactly what God does. Everything you have, every dollar you receive, every gift you're given, every talent you possess, every relationship you have is part of that Universal Energy, or Divine Love. Everything flows in and out of our lives coming and going, *and* the only thing you're asked to give for its presence in your life is 10% of what shows up. Not a bad deal.

Whenever you experience challenges in any area of your life, the first and best action is to take 10% of the income you receive and gratefully give it to people and places that feed your spirit. I can't stress this enough. Many people don't understand how they can tithe when they're struggling to make ends meet.

Tithing is the act of giving thanks for what you've already been given. You have this incredible business partner embedded in every fiber of your being (named Spirit, Divine Love, God, Goddess, Universe, Infinite Intelligence, whatever you choose) who has all the inside knowledge, energy and talent you'll ever need. Your business partner is ready, willing and able to share all this knowledge, energy and talent with you. In return, your business partner asks for only 10% of whatever you receive from using that knowledge, energy and talent.

Most business partners demand at least 50% for this kind of contribution. God demands *nothing* from you. God merely provides you with an opportunity to give back a portion of what you were given in the first place. If I offered to share with you everything I know about improving your life, asked you to pay me nothing, and told you that I would continue to share my knowledge if you passed along 10% of whatever income you received from that point forward, would it be worth it to pay 10%?

When you begin to acknowledge that you are one with this Divine Source, your awareness of what this truly means will expand. This Source supplies seed for the farmer and bread to eat. It also supplies you with all the seed you need—including divine inspiration, knowledge and action—and makes it grow and produce a rich harvest in every area of your life. All of this grows out of your generosity and gratitude. As you begin to give thanks with your tithe, you demonstrate you are ready for even greater good. Your "business partner" sees this expansion in your prosperity consciousness and opens your eyes to see the immense blessings of everything you have, do, give, receive and experience!

I encourage you to release past negativity, fear and attachment. Step out in faith with God, that inner Divine Love, as your business partner. You've learned the life lessons of negativity, fear and attachment well. Now it's time to move on to the graduate school of life, where you actively choose the positive in your life. Pull up a chair and sit yourself down firmly in life's prosperous flow.

Every day, remind yourself that you *deserve* everything and you *have* everything, because you *are* everything. Do this and you will become like a hyperactive person who takes time to sit still in a garden filled with hummingbird feeders. You will no longer see whispers of prosperity whizzing past you. You will see your prosperity manifest in all its glory.

Feel stuck and want to change something in your life? Then make today the day you start giving a percentage of your income to the source of your spiritual strength. It can even be as little as one percent. The *amount* doesn't matter. Only your commitment to yourself matters!

Stagnation is death. Circulation is life. Picture a swimming pool for a moment. You cannot keep a pool clean unless there is a way for the water to filter out and filter back in again, and you actively remove the debris that appears.

Our job is to keep the outlet and the inlet open—to receive and to give—and to take action to remove the debris. When we do, the stream of abundance continues flowing in and through us in infinite ways, both seen and unseen.

The only way to turn a belief into action is to express it in an outer, tangible form. Tithing turns the belief that everything comes from God into an active force. Our belief taps into that God Energy within us, bringing clearly into our minds the Truth that Divine Love IN us, AS us, IS us.

The True, Divine Model of Supply and Demand

I have absolute faith that anything can come to one who trusts in the unlimited help of the Universal Intelligence within, so long as one works within the law and always gives more to others than they expect and does it cheerfully and courteously.

—WALTER RUSSELL

We have two models in our lives: the scarcity model and the limitless model. The surest way to tap into the greater flow of abundance requires just two actions from you. First, let go of the scarcity model of supply and demand that says others must do without in order for us to have more. Second, enthusiastically embrace the limitless model.

Everything in the Universe consists of energy. In fact, matter is nothing more than rhythmic waves of light, thought and action patterned into what we call substance or matter. Light is the foundation of the Universe. And the secrets of creation lie in the wave, which is merely the physical expression of energy. Everything—absolutely everything—is part of this rhythmic flow of giving and receiving, part of a limitless supply of abundance.

The true nature of the Law of Supply and Demand is that there is no limit to any supply. Until we have a specific demand, however, we never tap the proper supply. Noted economists Henry Hazlitt, author of *Economics in One Lesson* and Paul Zane Pilzer, author of *God Wants You To Be Rich*, recognized the true spiritual nature of this law. As they discovered, when we have a demand the supply appears. Yet the supply that appears may not take the form we expect.

If we hadn't had a greater demand for gasoline in the 1970's, we never would have had a supply of fuel-efficient devices. As a result of these devices, the *amount* of gasoline we consume per vehicle is smaller now than it was 50 years ago. The amount of gasoline is not the same as the supply of gasoline. The *amount* of any resource is not the same as the *supply* of that resource. The amount of money you have on hand is not the same as the supply of money available to you.

Here's an example. One night, a farmer's four mules got loose and all were killed. Night after night, the farmer prayed for "a few more mules." Every morning, he took action on any idea he had to get new mules. Every day, the answer was the same: No new mules.

One day, he approached the owner of the general store about borrowing money so he could buy more mules. There was a store policy against lending money; instead, the owner agreed to let the farmer buy a tractor over time. All along, the farmer had been praying for more mules, when God had something bigger and better in store.

Always ask yourself, "What is my true demand? What is it I truly want?" The farmer kept asking for "a few more mules." The farmer's true demand, however, was not more mules; his true demand was to find a way to plant his crops.

By consistently taking the next step toward obtaining his new mules, he was able to find a new supply of power for planting his crops. His *supply* of planting power had changed from four mules to one tractor, but the *amount* of planting power had actually increased, because one tractor was far more powerful than four mules.

To firmly understand the true nature of the law of supply and demand, you must learn to trust that God has already provided for you. You must begin to recognize and acknowledge that you already have everything. You must have faith that the *Divine Law of Prosperity* has already provided what you hope for and desire, even when you can see no evidence this law is at work in your life.

Have faith in the *Divine Law of Prosperity* the same way you have faith in the Law of Gravity, even though you can see no evidence of that law working in your life.

Tithing is spiritual economics at work, the same way an apple falling from a tree is gravity at work. When you tap into the spiritual Source of the economy you will release that nothing, not even any downturn in the economy, has any power over you. This statement reflects a profound realization.

A friend recently reminded me of an incident that happened when my son was about 7 years old. My son was thirsty and picked up our friend's water bottle. The friend told him, "you don't want to do that—I'm sick." My son responded, "germs are real, but they have no power over me." He took a long drink of water, with no ill effects.

My friend was so impressed he taught this to *his* children and the amount of ill health in their house diminished greatly.

Whatever appears to be real—germs, shortages, economic stress, tight real estate markets—has no power over you.

When our rental home in Colorado sprung a leak in its foundation, we needed to move on short notice. Everyone around us kept bemoaning about how "tight" the rental market was and how impossible it was to find a good rental home. We looked at just three houses, fell in love with the third one and our application was accepted without fanfare. To us, there was no "tightness" in the rental market. There was simply Divine Love at work, IN us, AS us, drawing us and the homeowner together in perfect synchronicity.

In the biblical book of Mark (21:22), Jesus said, "If you believe, you will receive whatever you ask for in prayer." Every thought we have is a form of prayer. Our thoughts form our reality and thereby form whatever we have present in our lives. Is everything in your life a result of hard work or luck (good or bad)? What about everything you do not have?

Do you feel the absence of what you desire is due to some lack within you, a run of bad luck, or the devil running amuck in your life? Is everything *good* in your life a result of what *you* have done while everything you *lack* is a result of what *others* have done to you?

I ask you to consider the possibility that the *only* thing you really lack is trust. Have you ever primed a pump? If you have, then you know you can't simply walk up and start pumping away expecting water to flow out. It may flow out if the pump was recently primed, but if not, chances are nothing will come out. You need to *add* water if you want to *draw* water from the well. So, too, with tithing.

Benjamin Franklin said, "He that kills a breeding-sow, destroys all her offspring to the thousandth generation." When you don't give your tithe, you destroy all its offspring—all the divinely inspired ideas and abundance it contained.

Build a Foundation of Trust

How do you create trust in God, that Divine Love within you? Use whatever you have on hand to prime the pump and create a clear perception of the greater good in your life. Don't take what you've got, use it up and hope to find another source somewhere else down the road. Don't kill your breeding-sow. Nurture it with lovingkindness and thanksgiving, having faith in the abundance that flows forth from it.

In the biblical book of Hebrews (11:1), Paul said, "Faith is the substance of things hoped for, the evidence of things not seen." Faith is derived from the Latin *fidere*—to trust. To have faith means to trust in the promise, to have fidelity to the promise, to abide by the promise and to have a sincerity of your intentions.

Divine laws are laws that cannot fail. Understanding these laws requires you to have faith based on principle. I'm sure I frustrated many a math teacher with my endless questions, such as: "I know one plus one equals two, but *why*?" and "I know that the angles of a triangle always equal two right angles or 180 degrees, but *WHY*?"

Faith is the evidence of things not seen. Faith means knowing something works and putting it to work in our lives even when we don't know *why* it works. Many people know with *absolute certainty* that tithing works, although they do not know precisely *why* it works.

Tithing works because the laws of the Universal Spirit, the laws of God, are eternal, unchanging truths. One such truth is found in the Divine Law of Prosperity: *A lavish abundance already exists to meet your every desire. Ask for what you desire with the absolute certainty that it will be given to you.*

That's exactly what one woman who regularly tithes did. She sent me an email asking me to pray with her for her rapid certification in a new field. She sent off the email and moments later received word from her instructor that her certification had been approved. Although I hadn't yet read her email, she had received an instantaneous manifestation.

She had asked with complete faith that her request would be granted, because she believed in the prospering power of prayer. *My* actual prayers had nothing to do with the manifestation. I hadn't even read her email before her belief yielded fruit.

I urge you to continually rejoice and give thanks that you *have* (not that you will have) the desires of your heart. You already have the desire. Desire is the hope or promise of things unseen. Because you already have the desire, your good is already yours. Your good is merely in the realm of supply that is currently beyond your perception, out of sight. Through your tithes, you manifest that good in your life in a visible form.

If you win the lottery but never claim your prize, it does not make you less of a winner. It simply means that you didn't claim your good. You did not take the action necessary to claim your abundance and make it manifest in your life.

When you envy something that belongs to someone else or use it for your own benefit without permission, it does not make you more prosperous. It simply means you have claimed someone else's good. It is not the item they have—their spouse, their house, their car, their income, their possessions—that you desire.

What you desire is the *equivalent* of what your neighbor or your boss or your friend has, and you want to claim this equivalent for yourself. You want the love, the comfort and the joy *represented* by these things.

When you begin to understand the true nature of the Law of Supply and Demand you will begin to realize there is an unseen but unlimited supply of good for everyone. This is another part of the Divine Law of Prosperity: *No one needs to have less in order for someone else to have more.*

Affirm your rightful claim to the supply of love, comfort and joy that already exists in your life, rather than claiming the supply that belongs to another. Your supply will become visible in your life, according to the Divine Law of Prosperity, in Divine timing. Do not ask for success and then prepare for failure—prepare for the success.

I once needed to pay a $1,400 bill, but did not have all the money on hand the day before the bill was due. Rather than prepare for failure by rehearsing how I would convince my creditor to take my partial payment, I prepared for success by rehearsing how I would write out the check for the entire amount, address and mail the envelope, and let the creditor know the full payment was on its way.

Later that afternoon, I received a large book order that more than amply covered the amount due on the bill. I gave thanks, wrote out my tithe check, wrote out my check for the bill and called the creditor to alert them that the check was in the mail. Exactly as I had prepared to do before the money made itself visible to me. The knowledge that we already have everything brings what we desire into awareness.

Believe in what you desire. What happens if you test the theory of limitless supply in a water pump while not fully believing in it? You pour the water in and pump halfheartedly. Or you give up, affirming your "rightness" in the situation with statements such as "I knew it wouldn't work all along. What did you expect, with a pump this old?" All your efforts will have been in vain. The water level will drop back down into the pump, even if you were mere inches away from an outpouring of abundance the likes of which you have never seen.

If you trust, and keep taking action in faith, you will be rewarded with the water you seek. That first cup—which you willingly give back to the Source to "prime the pump"—will come back to you multiplied, filling up and spilling over like an endless waterfall until every container you have is filled to overflowing. The abundance you receive will provide you with enough to meet your every need—a luxurious bath, a hot pot of soup, filled canteens, irrigation of every growing thing in your life—and enough to share and to spare.

Your faith in the principle, your trust, is the power that exposes your good to you—the good that is right there, waiting for you. If you allow yourself to have faith and tithe without ceasing for one year, no matter what occurs, you will be more prosperous in all areas of your life. You will receive what you asked for, or you will be given the means to experience or achieve what you have asked for, *or something better,* as a man I met at a workshop in North Carolina discovered.

This man tithed and set his intention for his family's debt to be reduced to zero, affirming that he was open and receptive to "this or something better." Within 30 days, his company agreed to pay 100% of his tuition (which included weekend room and board) to attend Wake Forest's Executive MBA program. The cost was more than his family's debts and the payback over their lifetime is ongoing, because his salary continues to rise now that he has his MBA.

This man's demand was for the elimination of debt. The supply that he received was increased wisdom, which would result in increased income. *Receiving*—the act of taking or claiming your good—is as necessary to putting the Law of Supply and Demand into action as is *giving*. Especially when both are done with gratitude.

It has been said that the ultimate resource is people—skilled, spirited and hopeful people. When you want a promotion at work, you need to give forth an effort that shows you can do the job you want.

A woman working for me set her sights on a promotion. She began doing all tasks this new position required. She did these tasks—faithfully and joyfully—for six months before approaching me for a raise. I immediately and joyfully said yes to her request. The same can be true for any increase you seek. Your desires are met when you demonstrate that you are a good steward of everything you've already received.

Are you happy with what you already have, and do you use it wisely? If not, the Universe acts on the premise that you won't be happy with more if you can't be happy with what you already have.

Want something new or different in your life? How do you treat what you currently have? Do you treat it with loving kindness, giving thanks for what it provides, tithing of your time and attention, keeping it clean and in good running condition? Or do you treat it like a pile of junk, with disparaging words and neglect, while affirming that if you had a better one you would take better care of it? What about your car or phone? What about your health and relationships?

Tithing—giving thanks for what you currently have—starts in your mind. It starts with a change in attitude about everything and everyone that currently exists in your life. Giving thanks always begins as an inside job.

Session 3 Questions for Discussion

1. What common themes from last week's covenants have you included in your own covenant?

2. What unexpected good did you notice you received in the past week? Where did you perceive something this week as "good" that in the past you might have perceived as undesired?

3. Who in your life have you perceived as having judged what *you* did with *their* money?

4. Where do you judge what others do with things you give them?

5. Once you give a gift to someone, whose possession is it at that point?

6. What are you afraid of losing, or believe you do lose, when you give a gift that isn't properly appreciated?

Session 3 Activities (do one or more after Session 3)

1. **Dollar A Day Exercise:** Take a dollar every day this week and give it away to the third person you meet each day. Tell this person that you wanted them to have this gift of a dollar. Pay attention to both *their* reaction and *your* reaction. Write down everything that comes into your head about what you think they will do with the money, and how you feel about it.

2. Make a two column list. Mark the left column "inventory" and the right column "heart's desires." In the left column, write down an "inventory" of the good in your life—tangible and intangible. Everything you have, do or experience: your assets, your possessions, and the abundance that exists in your life, in your house of worship, in your relationships, in your spiritual growth, in your health, peace of mind and so on. On the right hand side, make a list of everything you desire to do, be or experience. Every day this week, before you take any action of any kind, look at the list and ask yourself: Is the action I'm about to take going to bring me closer to—or further from—one of the desires of my heart? Answer honestly, and then make a conscious choice to do or not do that action. Honor that choice, with-

out judging it as good or bad. Simply honor your choice. Write down what choices you make that bring you closer to your desires and what choices you make that bring you further from your desires. If you can, write down what thoughts went through your head as you made the choice. *Remember: this is a judgment free zone. Just observe and record.*

3. Use a fresh *Prosperity Tracker* to track the good that comes to you.

Now that you've completed Session 3, begin tithing 3%

Chapter Four

Before Session 4:

• Read Chapter 4

During Session 4:

• Discuss your experience doing
the activities after Session 3

• Discuss the questions at the end of this chapter

After Session 4:

• Begin tithing 4%

• Do one or more of the activities listed
at the end of this chapter

Is It Possible More Good Exists for You?

A true desire is not to have, but to be.

—ERIC BUTTERWORTH

How much abundance can you visualize coming into your life—realistically—in the next year? How about in the next 30 days? Do you base your answer strictly on the amount you know may come into your life from your paycheck, clients, tax refunds, consumer rebates, inheritances and the like? Or do you base your answer on your faith in what you desire, based on the knowledge that you already have everything?

A single mother called and left me a breathless message two days after attending my Saturday seminar. She spoke so quickly, the message sounded like Alvin and the Chipmunks had called, "Paula, I wanted to tell you about an AMAZING prosperity story that happened to me, and

I REALLY want you to call me back so I can share this AMAZING PROSPERITY STORY with you!"

It was nearly midnight, so instead of calling, I made a detour to my study. At every workshop, I teach people the truth about *tithing* and then I give everyone a blank postcard and ask them to write on it something they want to manifest in their lives during the next 30 days.

Some people write their desires for stronger relationships, physical healing, freedom from fear, increased prosperity in some form or another. This woman had written a single dollar figure on her postcard: $10,000. I went to bed that night fairly 'sizzling with zeal and anticipation,' eager to hear this woman's amazing prosperity story.

Her story was a perfect example of these principles in action. When she arrived home from work Monday evening, she began opening her mail. One envelope contained an unexpected check for $8,000. We joked that she still had another 28 days to manifest the additional $2,000.

In all seriousness, how was this manifestation of a completely unexpected $8,000 possible? Because this woman had learned how to get herself and her limited thinking out of the way so she could be in the flow—the Divine Flow, that is. Once she put herself in the prospering flow of abundance—tithing on every level of her life, including her thoughts, words, actions and treasures— she manifested nearly everything she desired within 48 hours of setting her intention.

Can you visualize an additional $10,000 coming into your life in the next 30 days? Can you, like this woman, hold the *possibility* in your mind? Or do you immediately dismiss it as impossible, simply because you can't *earn* that much money from your job in a month?

Skeptics who tithe with the firm belief that tithing does not work, are not tithing. They are merely giving money away with the expectation of getting something in return. This is not giving thanks. This is *conditional* giving. This is giving to get. This is bargaining. If I give you 10% of my income, then you must do x, y or z for me. It is the "what's in it for me" mentality.

True tithing is something different. Tithing means giving thanks. Giving in good faith and letting go of all expectations of the outcome of any events in our lives. It means letting go of the illusion that we control our level of prosperity and the amount of good in our lives.

It also means letting go of the illusion that we *can't* have something because we don't see *how* it is possible, or that we don't *already have* something because we can't see it.

If you've ever "lost" your car keys, in plain sight, you'll know exactly what I mean! It's like saying the angles of a triangle can't always add up to 180 degrees, because we can't see *why*.

What you want is your business. *How* it comes into your life—once you set the intention and give thanks for it and for the good that already exists in your life—is none of your business. Let me repeat that: *What you want is your business. How it comes to you is none of your business.*

We can't give 10% of our income away and somehow believe that everything will turn out the way *we* plan. The truth is, tithing often causes ripples and changes that may seem like the exact *opposite* of what you think you want, need and desire. Rest assured, even when things don't turn out the way we plan, things *always* turn out for our highest good. We just don't always *perceive* the good.

When I first started tithing, I was working my way up the corporate ladder. Within months, I was given notice that I was to be laid off from my well-paying editorial job. *Not* the result I expected!

I continued to tithe, even though my paychecks would soon disappear. I knew those paychecks were only one channel of my good, even though I had no idea when or where the next channel would appear. I released my expectation of the compensation I was going to *demand* from my employer. I didn't explode when the president of the company declared he didn't want to pay me any severance pay. I staying centered, tithing with my thoughts, waiting to see what he had in mind. He asked me to do several consulting jobs, which resulted in me receiving *twice* the amount my ego would have demanded. The omnipresent abundance of the Universe manifested in my life, despite appearances.

Is Your Glass Half Empty, Half Full or Overflowing?

My cup runneth over.

−THE BIBLE, BOOK OF PSALMS (23:5)

I sometimes begin workshops by holding up a glass of water, where the water level is as equidistant from the top of the glass as it is from the bottom. I then ask the age-old question: How would you describe this glass of water?

Some audience members say the glass is half-full. Others say it is half-empty. What is the truth?

The truth is: The glass is full to overflowing. Always.

The glass is half-full of water and half-full of air, and this air spills out, up, over, and into the Universal flow. It is only our limited thinking that sees the glass as half-full or half-empty. Like the glass, we are already full to the point of overflowing.

Universal good is unlimited and you can tap into it any time, manifesting the abundance in your own life, simply by opening up your mind to the *possibility* that more good exists for you.

Think outside the box. Look at everything that exists in your life already and embrace it wholeheartedly. See the good in every situation and know that even greater good is manifesting in your life. Then do your homework. Take action on your goals and make it a priority to begin systematically giving, no matter how small your tithe or how large your debts.

Never, ever, apologize for the size of your tithe. Never state words like "we only have" or "It's just this small amount" particularly when you're giving your full 10% tithe. When you give everything you have, when you let go of your attachment to your possessions and money and see yourself as the steward of the good in your life, you affirm that you rely on God as the Source of all abundance in your life. This opens you up to receive abundance from a multitude of channels, both expected and unexpected, because you are already fully immersed in that abundance.

Get Started Tithing

I first stumbled across the principle of tithing quite by accident. The events that laid the foundation for my discovery of tithing began in the early 1980's while I was living in New York City. One rainy Saturday, I sought shelter in a dinky basement bookstore where I discovered what I thought was a "get-rich-quick book."

The rain was letting up and I was in a hurry to get back to my apartment in-between downpours. I loved the title (*Prosperity Secrets of the Ages*), briefly glanced at the table of contents, and bought the book. Once I got home, I thumbed through the pages and discovered the book was filled with biblical references. At the time I was not very spiritually inclined, so I put the book down unread.

Every time I picked the book up over the years, I put it down again, unread. Over the course of 13 years I moved often, and even though I gave away many books during each move, this book by Rev. Catherine Ponder stayed with me.

One night, after a rough day at work, I couldn't sleep. I went to the bookshelf at two in the morning, looking for something to put me to sleep. *Prosperity Secrets of the Ages* caught my eye and I remember thinking, "Aha! *That* will do the trick!"

The next thing I knew the sun was coming up and I had read half the book, which discussed how a fascinating concept called tithing could improve your life forever. I was unhappy at work and in other areas of my life. I had recently ended a decade-long relationship. I bought my first home and moved to an area where I knew only one other person. I decided I had nothing to lose by testing the principles in the book. That morning, on my commute to work, I began doing the affirmation work and that week I began tithing.

I jumped in with both feet, tithing a full 10% immediately. Tithing was so foreign to me I initially gave away 10% of my income to various charities. At that point in my life, I wouldn't have known if something was feeding my spirit if it walked up and injected food right into my soul.

Soon, however, I found channels that fed my spirit and began tithing there. No matter what events unfolded, I always found myself with an inner peace of mind; an inner knowing, that some positive force was working behind the scenes, unfolding and moving me toward greater good in every area of my life.

When I first started tithing, I didn't know exactly how tithing worked any more than I knew how triangles worked so that their angles always added up to 180 degrees. I just knew that the divine laws that govern these principles were always at work in our lives. I encourage you to test the principles in this book for yourself and see what changes occur in your life.

Tithing offers a systematic way to create true and lasting abundance in all areas of your life. If you want to put tithing to the test for yourself, make a covenant with yourself to tithe for the next 12 months.

Starting today, commit to tithing 10% of all your income—and of every increase that comes to you—to wherever you are spiritually fed for one year. Then sit down and inventory everything you have: all your assets, your possessions, the abundance that is in your life in the form of relationships, spiritual growth, health, peace of mind, and so on. Next, make a list of all you feel you lack and all the desires of your heart. Note that I said all you *feel* you lack. The truth is, you do not lack anything. You already have everything. You only *fear* lack, and in your fear, you repel your good and keep it from your sight. Starting today, you're about to change that forever.

Put your lists away in a safe place and implement your covenant (in complete faith that the Universe has already provided for your every desire, no matter what outer circumstances occur, and no matter how strongly your faith is tested during the year. Stay the course, no matter what.

Faithfully give 10% of all your income—and 10% of every increase that comes to you—with a sense of thanksgiving. Tithe the first part of your time every day to that Infinite Intelligence that resides behind everything. Do these things and I guarantee one year from now you will feel more abundant and you will see how the desires of your heart have manifested.

When I first began tithing, I rotated my tithe systematically each week among four different charities. I observed my thoughts and feelings about tithing, including resentments that came up when my tithe wasn't acknowledged.

Gradually, as I learned more about tithing, I was drawn to tithe to spiritual places and ministers. I tithed to prosperity advisor Rev. Catherine Ponder (whose book got me on this path, and whose generous Foreword blessed this book). Then I began tithing to a Unitarian-Universalist church and a Unity church nearby in Annapolis, even though I'd never attended them.

Eventually, I began to see tithing as a way to give thanks, to give a "glad offering" to God, as a way of showing my gratitude for all the blessings in my life. I stopped seeing the money I was giving as an obligation or a charitable donation or an effort to "get" ten-fold back. Instead, I started seeing my tithe as a blessing—to me. The larger my tithe was, the more I knew I'd been blessed that week. Anytime the 10% I gave had increased, the 90% I had left was that much more. As my spirituality grew, I was guided to tithe wherever I was being spiritually fed, and I began giving my tithe to places that nourished my soul each week.

Where Should You Tithe?

*Bring to the storehouse a full tenth of what you earn
so there will be food in my house. Prove me now,
herewith,' says the Lord Our God. 'If I will not open
you the windows of heaven and pour you out
a blessing so big it cannot be contained."*
—THE BIBLE, BOOK OF MALACHI (3:10)

Every now and then, a new subscriber to my newsletter (www.paulalangguthryan.com), will write me and chastise me for perpetuating the notion that you can "give your tithe to anywhere you want." These well-meaning souls generally refer to the above scripture from the book of Malachi as evidence that all tithes are to be given to your local church.

Some aspects about tithing have been widely misunderstood by religious institutions, leaders and followers, which is partly why this book evolved. Some people believe we are obligated to give our tithes directly to religious organizations. Others believe we are not blessed by our tithes, but are only blessed by what we give above and beyond our tithes. It is true that you are not blessed by simply giving away 10% of your money, which may be where this belief began.

You are blessed when your 10% is a *true tithe*—when you are using your tithe to give thanks for the abundance you have been given.

Where should you tithe? As the scripture says, tithe to "the storehouse." The storehouse consists of all the people and places that spread the word of God, of Spirit, of Allah, all the people and places who make you feel immersed in Spirit, those people who *inspire* you.

Bring your tithe to those people and places that minister to your spirit, regardless of their theological credentials. Where you worship may or may not be where you find your spiritual inspiration. If you are spiritually fed where you worship each week, then that is *exactly* where you should be tithing. Your tithe allows the people who provide you with spiritual inspiration to feed themselves, which in turn allows them to continue to feed your spirit and the spirit of others whom they have not yet met. Your tithe allows them to send *their* tithe out into their local community and into the world at large. Your tithe guarantees there is "food in my house," as the scripture says.

In Jewish temples, no collections are taken at services. Each temple is self-supporting through the tithes of its members, with one exception: they charge a fee for admission to High Holy Day services. As we move beyond the obligatory tithe and reclaim the true giving nature of the tithe, one day I see even these services becoming available to all who desire to attend them, regardless of financial ability.

Many people have a strong negative emotional reaction to tithing, because we have largely strayed from the original meaning. Tithing gives thanks for the blessings we've received and demonstrates that we are putting Spirit first in our lives.

Tithing has gotten a bad rap. Some religious institutions try to calculate their annual budgets based on their members' projected contributions, instead of trusting God to supply them with what they desire. This is why they try to convince their congregations that the tithe is mandatory and offerings are optional. This fear-based mentality (masquerading as "fiscal responsibility" or "sound money management") keeps organizations in a perpetual state of lack.

To raise greater funds for an organization, you must first raise the consciousness of those within it. Peace of mind, as Napoleon Hill often said, is the greatest wealth of all. Peace of mind is the true wealth that underlies all material wealth.

Help people see they have an opportunity—not an obligation—to bring their tithes into the storehouse to perceive God's blessings.

When you tithe, it may be appropriate to tell the person or organization why you're tithing to them. Or you may want to send a note that says "thank you for feeding my spirit" or any other kind words that come to mind. On occasion, you may find it better to tithe anonymously.

Years ago I learned of an accident that had happened to a local family. Their loss reminded me of my good fortune. I tithed anonymously with a note telling the mother to use the money for something to feed her own spirit, so she would have the strength and courage to be there for her children after her husband's death. Because we lived in a very small town I was concerned the woman might be embarrassed by the gift, so I sent it anonymously. I didn't want pride to prevent her from accepting the gift.

When you tithe, give your tithe with no concern as to whether or not your tithe is "needed." It's easy to make the snap decision that your tithe *is not* needed if the place where you are spiritually fed reports it has received an abundance of tithes, or *is* needed because the place where you are spiritually fed reports a great need. Do not allow yourself to be distracted by fearful thinking that they do, or don't, need the money as much as some other place might.

Always give to wherever you are spiritually fed, regardless of perceived need. Give your tithe out of a sense of thanksgiving, not out of a sense of charity. Divine Love works through the people around us to feed us. Infinite Intelligence knows the true need and heart's desires of all.

I once was clearly guided to give my tithe directly to my minister, rather than to the church I attended. I was confused at first, but that Voice for God was very insistent that I should tithe directly to my minister. I did not understand the reason at the time. I even went so far as to engage in a mental debate with God Within Me about the whole thing, before eventually conceding and tithing directly to my minister.

My minister later told me my tithe arrived just as she was trying to figure out how to pay for a plane ticket she had booked so she could travel to Florida to be with her husband who was having a health challenge. The amount of my tithe was *exactly* the amount of the airline ticket.

I never again doubted where I should send my tithe. Since then I've always sent my tithe to where I was spiritually fed that week or that day.

The Mechanics of Tithing

What we give multiplies and circulates back to us through the dynamic law of giving and receiving. Not only the time, talent, dollars and love that we give, but also the resentment, the smallness, the bitterness, will do the same.

—Mary Manin Morrissey

Tithing is about giving thanks for what you have already received and for what you know is all around you. As I've said before, tithing is not about giving to get. However, the more fully you tithe, the more blessings wind up being bestowed upon you. This is the Universal promise to you. How much you actually tithe is up to you. What limit do you want to place on the opportunities in your life?

The ideal 10% tithe is from your gross income, but not everyone can comfortably embrace that idea from the start. Tithe on whichever—gross or net—you can cheerfully, willingly and joyfully tithe. I encourage you to start with 10% of your net income after taxes but before retirement plan contributions and the like. (This program will help you gradually increase your comfort level around tithing a full 10%.)

A true tithe for a business owner would be 10% of gross profits (revenue minus cost of goods sold). A tithe on *net* profits would be approximately 3% of gross profits. If it's more comfortable, start there and work your way up. Each quarter, increase your tithe 1% of gross profits, until your company is tithing a full 10% from gross profits.

This next bit is a sticky subject for some. Many people uncover hidden guilt when they ponder the process I'm about to describe. I encourage you to sit with whatever comes up as you read this: *Borrowed money is income.*

If you borrow money, tithe 10% of the money you borrow. Income is income no matter what form it takes or what channel it arrives from. If you live beyond your means and use credit to purchase goods and services, and you want to get out of debt, begin to tithe on the amount you "borrow" from creditors. Include the amount of credit you borrowed as if it were actual income you received, since you've already exchanged that credit for goods or services you desired. If you charge $1,000, tithe $100. Work up to a full 10% as you're guided, tithing joyfully and willingly—and watch your debt begin to disappear.

Now, let's talk about tax refunds. If you're tithing from your net income (after taxes and other deductions are taken out), make sure you tithe from your tax refunds as well. This will eventually make it possible for you to tithe from your gross income.

A woman felt like she had created a financial imbalance after not tithing on her state tax refund. She was afraid to spend her federal tax refund without taking care of her tithe first. She realized she was operating out of fear, because she felt like she was impeding the good in her life. She used her federal tax refund to pay both her tithes and immediately found relief from her anxiety.

When you tithe on your net income, your income tax refunds represent money you haven't paid a tithe on yet. Give thanks for the Universal stream of abundance by tithing 10% from your tax refunds. Tithe as a way to say "Thank you, God" for your home, for all the blessings that have been bestowed upon you, for everything that has come to you and all the opportunities revealed to you during the previous year.

Eventually, you will be able to tithe on the tax as well, and you will suddenly find you're tithing from your gross after all. The person who plants a little will have a small harvest, but the person who plants a lot will have a big harvest.

Give as you have decided in your heart to give. Do not give when you are sad or afraid. Do not give because you feel forced to give. Do not give out of habit or obligation.

God loves the "cheerful giver"—the person who gives happily. Divine Energy can give you more blessings than you can possibly imagine—if you make room for Infinite Intelligence to work in your life. When you actively take part in giving your full 10% tithe, you will always have plenty of everything and enough to give to every good work.

What Stops You From Tithing?

However small your capabilities may seem at present to you, you are just as much a necessity to God as the most brilliant intellect, the most thoroughly cultured person in the world. Remember this always, and act from the highest within you.

—H. Emilie Cady

Many people believe they simply cannot afford to tithe. They believe their income comes from their hard work, and not from the Universe in the first place. The thought of tithing fills them with fear. If you find yourself in this situation, the exercises below will help you ease into giving thanks with your full tithe. In fact, you're already doing these exercises, by doing the study group activities in this book.

I'm talking about *gradual tithing*—starting with 1% and working up to a full 10% tithe. If you haven't found the courage to begin tithing I encourage you to do one of the following:

1. Tithe daily for 21 days. Just for the next 21 days. Psychologists say that it takes 21 days to make something a habit. If you receive $10 on Monday, tithe $1 on Tuesday. If you receive $1,000 on Tuesday, tithe $100 on Wednesday. Tithe 10% of any income you receive the previous day—just for 21 days. Develop the habit of daily tithing. See how far your remaining 90% goes those three weeks. After 21 days, if you still don't feel comfortable tithing a full 10%, drop back to a comfortable percentage. As your comfort level grows, increase your tithe.

2. Transform the *amount* you currently tithe into a *percentage*. This is a great exercise if you currently give set amounts to your place of worship or to people, places and organizations that feed your spirit. Change your thinking about the amount you're giving. Figure out what percentage you're giving based on the amount you're currently giving. Let's say you routinely give $10 weekly to wherever you are spiritually fed and you receive $500 weekly. A full 10% tithe would be $50 weekly. Giving $10 weekly means you're already tithing 2%!

Make a covenant with yourself that you are now tithing whatever percentage matches your current giving. Begin consciously tithing that percentage from here on out. In the above example, you would commit to giving 2% of your income from all channels every week.

If someone gives you a $100 gift card this week, your *income* this week would be $600. Your 2% *tithe* for this week would now be $12.

When you consistently give the same amount regardless of your income, you block your flow of abundance. Ten dollars is always going to be ten dollars. Giving the same percentage of your income systematically, gives you a concrete way to see the greater abundance in your life. Put it to the test. Track your abundance. Track your daily income and gifts. Use the *Prosperity Tracker* at the back of this book. Each month, make it a goal to increase your tithing percentage. Seeing the evidence of your increased prosperity is a powerful motivator!

Many people tell me they want to tithe but they are so in debt they can't even meet their current obligations. How in the world can they tithe if they can't even pay their bills? Believe it or not, the quickest way to get *out of debt* is to tithe your full 10% while you're *in debt*.

A woman attended my *Break the Debt Cycle* workshop and set her intention to be debt free within a year. She created a *Debt-Buster Strategy* that would have her completely out of debt within three years. She then implemented her plan and began systematically paying her tithes *and* paying off her debts. Thirteen months later, she was completely debt-free and even had a new car. If I had told her *how* her intention would come true, she says she would never have believed me.

If you're in debt or someone is in debt to you, start tithing by giving thanks for the trust that created the original financial transaction. Write out your tithe check and give thanks for the limitless Source from which your current conditions came from. In this way, you begin to form the habit of blessing everything you already have.

A woman applied for a loan to pay off credit card debt to reach her intended desire of being debt free, but the loan was declined. She had taken herself out of the flow of abundance and tried to take control of the reins herself, learning an important lesson in the process: you can't get out of debt by borrowing money. Borrowed money is still debt.

Infinite Intelligence will give you abundant ideas on how to get yourself moving on your debt reduction if this is an area that needs work in your life. Hold the consciousness of what your life will look like when you're debt free. Take action toward actively paying off debt day by day, even a few cents or dollars a day, through the choices you make with the way you spend your money. At the same time, give thanks for everything you receive, by paying your tithe before you pay anything else.

Your goal of being debt-free will manifest much quicker when you concentrate on prosperity and abundance principles than when you concentrate on chasing new sources of income. *Be still and know.* Knowledge of the next right and perfect financial step will be revealed to you in the stillness, where you connect your mind with the Universal Mind of Infinite Intelligence.

Many people contact me because they don't currently have a steady stream of income and they want to know how they are supposed to tithe 10% of nothing. Or they vow their commitment to tithing—the minute they receive some income. The best way to create a new stream of income is to willingly give before you receive. Give on faith, like Jacob, that your blessings will be poured out for you.

Start tithing on whatever amount you have on hand. Tithe 10% of whatever is in your change jar, in drawers and between couch cushions.

Tithe 10% of the cash in your home and 10% of the amount in your savings and investment accounts, especially if you've never tithed before. Demonstrate your willingness to tithe on what you've already received. Doing so opens up untold doors to receiving the greater good that is already yours.

We live in a consumer age, where increased income usually leads us to greater spending, and I get many questions from people who struggle to save money while practicing the art of tithing. Financial experts direct us to "pay ourselves first" by setting aside 10% of the income we receive.

If you're paying your 10% tithe, and then setting aside 10% in savings, how on earth would you *ever* survive on 80% of your income? Acknowledge your fear, and then put in place a systematic way to build your savings while continuing your commitment to tithe. As your consciousness expands through the art of tithing, you'll find it's easier to make the leap to living on 80% of what you previously lived on.

Until then, start gently. For one week, tithe 10% of your income to your spiritual source, and set aside 1% for your savings. The second week, tithe 10% and set aside 2% for your savings. The third week, tithe 10% and save 3% and so on. In ten weeks, you'll have increased your income—and your savings—to the point where you are effortlessly tithing your full tithe while also setting aside a full 10% in your savings. If adding increased savings each week is too scary, start saving 1% for a month and go up from there, increasing your percentage monthly.

In our study guide, you'll begin tithing 4% at the end of this chapter. See how it feels to put an additional 1% into savings, just for today.

"Can't Afford" and "Costs Too Much"

The nature of gratitude helps dispel the idea
that we do not have enough, that we will never
have enough, and that we ourselves are not enough.

—Wayne Dyer

Your words are powerful. You create your world by your thoughts and words, which is why it's important for you to know what you are really creating when you say or think *I can't afford* something.

What you're really saying is, *I'm not worthy* and *I'm not good enough.* Your words reflect how you value yourself. What do you believe you can't afford to do? You believe you can't afford what you want. What does this belief say about the importance you place on what you want?

I can't afford is an excuse. Blunt, I know. But true. You *can* afford to do anything you desire. Having what you desire, however, might take a little more effort than you're used to expending. A more accurate statement would be, "I'm not willing to pay the cost." Be honest with yourself. Are you willing to pay the cost? Or is the payoff of complaining about the current state of your life more appealing having what you want?

That costs too much is another one of these fake statements. When you truly desire something, nothing can keep you from finding a way to have it or create it. The next time you hear yourself say, "That costs too much," stop and analyze what you're really saying. What is it you're afraid to pursue for yourself? What price *are* you willing to pay for what you want? Do you want to pay off your debt and still go away on vacation? Then connect yourself with the Divine Flow. Give your full tithe *and* allow Spirit to bring your desire into manifestation.

When my family wanted to go on vacation to Florida years ago, we set an intention to spend two weeks at the beach. Through Divine Flow, we wound up house-swapping with Florida friends, and even had use of each other's cars while we were on vacation. Our only expenses were our airfare and the cost of the food and activities we enjoyed during our trip.

A similar thing happened the following winter when we set an intention to have access to a cabin for the ski season. We set our intention, and again—through Divine Flow—a family who wanted to gift coaching sessions to their grown children asked if I would trade sessions for unlimited use of their vacation house outside Breckenridge.

That same Divine Flow is active in *your* life, right now. You have within you the power to start creating what you truly want—today. Start building the life of your dreams, right now. The fact is, the only thing you cannot afford to do is to live your life with a mindset that supports you having *less* than the life of your dreams. It's time to stop playing little; stop "belittling" yourself and start being BIG!

To help you ingrain this new way of thinking and speaking you'll find a page at the back of this book which I lovingly call *The Abundance Zapper.* This handy sheet includes sixteen common words and phrases to eliminate from your vocabulary (with positive replacements).

Session 4 Questions for Discussion

1. What did you discover about why you believe it matters what other people do with their money? How does what they do with their money relate to you?

2. What are you afraid you will lose if you let go of your attachments?

3. What actions have you been guided to take since Session 3?

4. What expectations are you having about the outcome? What will happen if your expectations aren't met? What *expectancies* could you have about situations instead of *expectations*?

5. What is "your true demand"—what is it you *really* want? If you say you want money, what do you want the money *for*? If you say you want a relation-

ship, improved health, a better job—what do you want those things *for*? Get specific about your true heart's desires, so you can easily recognize them when they appear.

6. What have been the "offspring" of your tithes since Session 3? What results did you see (share your Prosperity Tracker).

7. In what areas can you be a better steward of something you want anew in your life? How can you be a better steward of your current attitudes, job, relationships, health, money, house, car, etc.?

Session 4 Activities (do one or more after Session 4)

1. Write your tithe check first, before you spend any other money. If you receive money on a daily basis, write out a tithe check every day, based on what you received the previous day, so you get in the habit of writing your tithe first, without fear of there being "not enough" left over.

2. Ask everyone you know to help you "watch your mouth" by pointing out whenever you use any of the words or phrases on the *Abundance Zapper* at the back of the book. Use the replacement language instead. You can download a full-size copy of the *Abundance Zapper* at http://paulalangguth ryan.com/free.

3. Review your intention and this week, practice "seeing it right." If you have a health challenge, instead of focusing on what is wrong, or what needs healing, focus on the truth of who you are: whole, vibrant, alive. See the parts of your body, even the smallest parts, as being truly whole, as they are in Truth, rather than in your perception. See your lungs strong and clear, see your relationships in perfect harmony, see your car in perfect working order, etc. Continue to hold each person's intention in prayer.

4. Use a fresh *Prosperity Tracker* to track the good that comes to you.

Now that you've completed Session 4, begin tithing 4%

Chapter Five

Before Session 5:

• Read Chapter 5

During Session 5:

• Discuss your experience doing
the activities after Session 4

• Discuss the questions at the end of this chapter

After Session 5:

• Begin tithing 5%

• Do one or more of the activities listed
at the end of this chapter

Become One With Life's Prosperous Flow

There should be no distasteful tasks in one's life.
Love anything you must do.
Do it not only cheerfully but lovingly
and the very best way you know how.

—WALTER RUSSELL

Creating the inner change that leads to your expanded prosperity consciousness may seem like a daunting task. So much of our world's abundance is currently trapped inside of fear, apathy, resentment, hatred and so on. You may, in fact, find some areas of your life distasteful.

Are there bills you haven't paid, because you're afraid once you do an emergency will come up for which you might need the money? Are you still in a relationship you've outgrown, because you're afraid you won't find anyone else who loves you or you're afraid of being alone? Are you clinging to old habit patterns that have outlived their usefulness, because you're afraid of the unknown changes that might occur if you give them up? Are you not pursuing a lifelong dream, because you are afraid of what you will need to release in your current life? Do you work every day at a job that is meaningless to you, because you believe your job is merely a means of paying your bills? Do you have a pattern of not liking people for certain reasons or behaviors? Or are there other fears holding you back?

Tithing gives you an opportunity to gently observe how your fears hold you back from achieving your highest good. Just look. Observe. No need to actually make any changes right now. Just simply take the time to examine different areas of your life and recognize where you may be reacting out of fear, instead of actively embracing your abundance. Identify your fears if you want to experience a more fully abundant life.

Now, let's examine how you define a fully abundant life. How do you define *abundance*? What is it you truly desire? Are you seeking a specific dollar amount, or what you *truly* want? There really is a difference.

A woman once asked me to affirm that a million dollars was now coming to her. I asked her what she wanted the million dollars *for*, and she said a home. Instead of affirming the million dollars, I asked her to walk me through what the property looked like and what the house looked like, inside and outside. I told her I would affirm the right and perfect home coming to her, as she desired.

A single mother of two small children was struggling with how she would ever find a home for the amount of the subsidized rent she was able to pay. I asked her to write down exactly what she wanted in a home, and let go of the fear that she would not be able to afford what she wanted. I asked her to have faith that what she desired would come to her. She called in amazement a few weeks later to delightedly share that the right and perfect house was now hers, at the rent she could afford.

When you're in what you perceive to be a distasteful situation, particularly a financial situation, it's easy to believe *lack of money* makes you uncomfortable. Not true. The discomfort actually comes from your attachment to the money you *do* have. Maybe you're afraid of not getting the *right* value for your money, so you withhold your tithes or resent the fees others charge you. Maybe you're attached to seeing tangible proof of work, so you *give* money to someone like a musician in *exchange* for a concert, rather than as a "thank you" for their music.

Many people make this mistake with their tithes. They "give to get" instead of giving as a means of saying "thank you," because someone fed their spirit. When you give to get with your tithe, you're putting *yourself* first. When you give thanks with your tithe, you are putting *Source* first in all areas of your life.

Here's a fun exercise to do the next time you think about paying someone a compliment. Usually when we give someone a compliment, we point out something wonderful they did, which then results in *them* saying "thank you" to us. Instead, say "thank you" to them. Tell a singer, for instance, "thank you for the gift of your amazing voice and music." You'll find you're suddenly giving in gratitude with your words, rather than giving to get a *thank you* back.

Tithing releases you from the emotional struggle surrounding financial and non-financial issues around giving and receiving. Tithing teaches you how to release your attachments to the abundance in your life. When you release your attachment to everything that comes and goes, you give your abundance permission to flow more freely.

Imagine the flow of prosperity as water flowing through a garden hose. Being attached to the prosperity in your life puts a kink in the hose and cuts off the flow. Release the kink and the water flows freely. Release your attachment to events in your life and the good in your life flows freely. Your attachment is all in your mind; it begins and ends with your thoughts and feelings about giving and receiving.

Tithing also allows you to sit peacefully in the quicksand of your financial worries and observe your thoughts and feelings. By giving thanks for everything that occurs in your life, you begin to see how your thoughts either draw greater good to you or repel your good. When people share their good with you, it is because they are responding to the energy you have sent out that announces you are worthy and deserving of having good come to you.

Everyone and everything taps into this energy flow and willingly acts in ways that bless you, in direct proportion to the way you willingly take action to bless everyone and everything in your life. As this begins to happen, all you need to do is trust. Trust the Universe to provide you with everything you need when you need it. Continue doing the work you do, because it is your mission to do so, not because it's the only means to make your mortgage or rent payment.

Consider the mission of Satish Kumar, author of *Path Without Destination*. He walked 8,000 miles from India to Washington, DC on a mission of peace in the 1980s. He carried no money with him on his journey. He trusted the Universe to provide him with food, shelter and safe passage across the oceans.

Even when surrounded by discomfort, he did not bemoan the job he had undertaken, or throw up his hands and quit in disgust. He quietly continued on his journey. He tithed of his time, his treasure and his abilities, and the Universe responded by opening up untold channels of good for him to accomplish his desire to raise the global *peace* consciousness. Unwittingly, along the way, he also raised the global *prosperity* consciousness of every person he met.

You too have it within you to raise the world's consciousness. Does anyone owe money to you? If so, I encourage you to use the art of tithing as a way to clear up any outstanding debt owed you. Whenever you feel someone "owes you," financially or otherwise, you're stopping the flow of your prosperity. Resentments you hold onto for unpaid debts impede the flow of your good. Reaffirm the trust you placed in that person when you first extended credit to them. You believed, you trusted, in their ability to grow and prosper. Begin to see this person not as a deadbeat, unwilling or unable to repay you, but instead as someone who is growing more prosperous and giving every day.

Release the obstacle you've put in front of the trust you originally placed in this person. Write a letter or making a simple phone call that says: "I've decided the money I gave you is a gift, and not a loan. Therefore, I now free you from any obligation to repay that money. I hope you will do the same for someone who owes you money." With all your heart, decide that this was indeed a gift.

Once you do this, amazing things will begin to happen. Years ago, I lent a friend $2,500. After I while, I realized I probably would never see the money again. I wrote the above note, and released her from the debt. I soon received a generous book order for several thousand dollars.

Releasing my attachment to the *form* my abundance took, I made it possible for even greater good to come to me from elsewhere. Over the years, this same friend tithed probably close to ten times the original amount, sharing her time and abilities with me.

A Multitude of Blessings

Good, the more communicated, more abundant grows.

—JOHN MILTON

Most people think of a financial tithe as something monetarily paid from their primary stream of income, such as their paycheck. They never give the practice of tithing another thought. Don't limit God to one income stream or you will forever be emotionally tied to the income from that channel. What if you get laid off, fired, or the company goes under? What if your best client stops buying goods or services from you?

As long as you think your abundance is limited to this one channel, you will forever be fearful of losing your income stream, until you open your mind to tithing from all financial channels. When you become open to giving thanks and tithing from all the abundance that comes into your life, you will stay open to *receiving* abundance from all channels in your life. The same applies when you tithe of your time, your abilities and your treasures, as well as your words, thoughts and actions.

When you tithe of your time, you often get back more time and the time of others. When you tithe of your abilities, you get access to the abilities of others. When you tithe of your treasures, you receive more abundance in all areas.

Be on guard against subconscious roadblocks you set up. If you find yourself rationalizing why it's not necessary to give your tithe, especially in non-monetary ways, check in to see what's scaring you.

Notice where you're hesitant to tithe of your thoughts, words or actions. You may fear someone taking advantage of you, or you may not trust someone to be supportive or not hurt you. These fears can show you unhealed relationship issues from the past that are ready to be healed. If relationship issues are something you want to explore, I recommend reading my book *Manifest the Perfect Mate* (G&D Media, 2021).

When you're hesitant to tithe of your treasures, old money issues may be coming up. Our relationships with money are very complicated and are based—consciously or subconsciously—on our childhood money beliefs. If you are looking to explore your money issues, I recommend reading my *Heal Your Relationship with Money* workbook. One common money issue that surfaces for many people is *control.*

We are uncomfortable not *knowing* the tithe we give is blessing us. Unlike money we send to a creditor or vendor—which immediately reduces or pays off a bill—a tithe generally has no direct, tangible result we can immediately point to as evidence of our prosperity.

Likewise, we may tithe words of kindness to someone and receive a short-tempered reply in return. It is tempting to throw in the towel when this occurs, but I encourage you to let go of the immediate appearances and continue to tithe of your thoughts, words and actions.

You may not always recognize the form abundance takes when what you are receiving is not actual dollars and cents. That's okay. The next step toward receiving greater abundance is to acknowledge your abundance in whatever form it takes, whether you're giving or receiving that abundance.

Start observing the many ways people have tithed to you recently, other than directly giving you money. Pay attention to how you have tithed to others without directly giving them money. Then consciously look to see how you can tithe to others in the future.

A woman shared with me a technique for remembering her daily abundance. She tracks her income, expenses and gifts she receives every day in a little notebook. If someone buys her lunch, she records the cost of the lunch as a gift. If she finds a dime on the sidewalk, she records the ten cents as a gift. If someone offers to carpool with her and she doesn't have to drive that day, she records the money saved in gas and automobile wear and tear as a gift. If she's out shopping and the item she intended to buy is on sale, she records the difference between the regular price and the sales price as a gift. Whenever she receives a hug, she records how much the hug meant to her as a gift. She carefully records a monetary value for each gift, so she can clearly see her abundance.

While I was running errands one day, I decided to try this gift-recording technique. The results were astonishing. First, I dropped off a prescription at the pharmacy and got free lollipops. Value: 25-cents. Then I went to lunch and freely offered some marketing advice to the restaurant owner, who gifted me with a free $15 lunch and two free loaves of bread ($7). Back at the pharmacy, the expensive prescription was filled generically —a gift of $70. At the grocery store two items on my list were "buy one, get one free;" $6 worth of free groceries. And last, but not least, I got perhaps the oddest gift of all: a free pap smear. Don't ask.

As I have said, we don't always recognize the form our abundance takes! My total gifts for the day were $208.25—not a penny of which came in the form of legal tender.

What overlooked gifts have you received in your life today or during the past month? One man tithed an article to my newsletter, plus introductions to people and organizations that might benefit from my work. A friend once tithed a blue blazer to me, among other wonderful gifts. Friends tithed their homes to me for silent writing retreats. Others tithed their time and their abilities, helping me with seminar mailings, making me meals, watching my dog, bringing me breakfast, driving me around town, buying groceries, proofreading, transcribing, chauffeuring me to and from airports and speaking engagements, offering legal or financial advice, sending me inspirational articles, providing technical support, giving me massages or making me laugh.

Start keeping a gift record, and see the vast abundance in your life. You can start right here, reading this book. Count as a gift the uplifting spiritual messages you receive as you read along. In addition, start keeping track of all the ways you tithe to others. When you tithe—regardless if you're tithing of your finances, time, talent, treasures, words, thoughts or actions—don't second guess *why* you're extending this love.

Free Up Your Trapped Prosperity

The only thing that stands between a man and
what he wants from life is often merely the will
to try it and the faith to believe it is possible.
—Ralph Marston

Always listen to your intuition—your inner voice—and tithe of your time, talent and treasures accordingly. Don't tithe where you think you *should* tithe or try and rationalize whether or not you are tithing in the right place. Don't wait for someone else to tithe of their words, thoughts or actions first. Let Spirit guide you to spontaneously give your tithes wherever you are spiritually fed.

A church found its expenses were exceeding their income, and their savings were being depleted, even though the church continued to give away 10% of all its income. I soon discovered what was obstructing their Divine Flow. They were tithing routinely without much thought as to where their tithes went. They had created a "tithing schedule" and were sticking to their schedule, rather than giving thanks to places that fed their spirit that week. They had begun to tithe to certain organizations out of a sense of obligation and not where they were necessarily being spiritually inspired. A few minor adjustments were all it took to get them back on track, building the church home of their dreams.

Are you tithing out of obligation, duty, or habit, or are you tithing where you are spiritually helped, inspired and fed *today*?

Many people give money to spiritual organizations and various charities for years, seeing no positive results in their lives. They tithe with the underlying sense that somehow they are bribing God to bring them money. They are in essence *giving to get*. This is a common tithing trap into which people fall. Your tithe is not intended as a bribe to the Universe. Your tithe is a gift, freely given back to the Source of all good as a way of giving thanks for all you've experienced.

Another common trap is tithing to a religious institution where you no longer attend or where you aren't spiritually fed. Are you tithing from habit, instead of joy? Are you tithing because you don't know where else to tithe, or because you believe you are supposed to tithe to your place of worship? Are you tithing because you made a commitment to tithe through a stewardship program? Are you tithing, even unconsciously, in order to look good or prosperous in the eyes of other congregants or to get accolades for being a consistent donor?

A minister once shared her gratitude that I was conducting a prosperity in-service for her board members. She was grateful, she said, because it appeared some board members weren't tithing to the church on a regular basis. Imagine her surprise when I told her that *where* her board members tithed was none of her business!

When you practice the art of tithing, be sure you're tithing to your spiritual Source. One way to get into the habit of tithing to your spiritual Source is to spend 30 days tithing on the spot to anyone who feeds you spiritual food that day. Don't save your tithe up for the Sabbath; God's Universal energy does not dwell only in a place of worship any more than it dwells in any other specific place. God is present everywhere, always.

What you need and want in order to do the things you desire doesn't come from your paycheck or your clients or your investment income. As scary as the thought may be, your financial good may not come tomorrow from the same people, places and things where it has come from in the past. It may, and probably will, come in a different form than you've ever seen before. But your abundance will come, and it will come when you need it, if you release the fear that what you need and want won't be there, and you step forward in faith.

There is One Source for your security. Whatever you wish to call that Source—God, Infinite Intelligence, Light, Divine Love, Great Spirit—is up to you. Whatever name you give your spiritual Source, don't withhold your good from the channels that connect you to that spiritual Source. Give your tithe joyously, give your tithe gladly, and it will come back to you tenfold, hundredfold, even thousand-fold.

Let Go of Your Guilt Gifts

It is the thought that counts.

—Anonymous

Many people think giving and receiving are part of the same cyclical flow of energy. The truth is something more: Giving and receiving are *exactly* the same thing. When you receive, you say "thank you," right? What is it you're really doing when you give? When you give someone a birthday present, you're saying "thank you for being born!" When you give someone a retirement present, you're saying "thank you for all your years of service." When you give your spouse an anniversary gift, you're saying "thank you for putting up with me all these years."

You cannot be a cheerful, joyful, loving, willing, grateful *giver* until you learn how to be a cheerful, joyful, loving, willing, grateful *receiver*, and vice versa.

Yes, you may be given gifts you don't need or want. Begin to see yourself as the *steward* of these gifts, a stop on the journey to their forever home. You are here to receive the gifts gratefully and to keep them in the storehouse until it is time for you to give them away. If it helps, instead of thinking of it in terms of "giving and receiving," think of it as "giving and *experiencing*."

Receiving may often be more about the *experience* than the *keeping* of what is given. Here's an example from my own life. My mother and I always had vastly different tastes in clothes. One year, my mom fulfilled a lifetime goal: traveling around Alaska for six months. For my birthday that year, she sent me a card with a beautiful note and a bright yellow t-shirt emblazoned with two polar bears and the word *Alaska* across the bottom. My sister Rebecca, with whom I graciously share my birthday month, received a similar t-shirt; hers was deep blue with two doe-eyed seals.

My mom and sister caught up with each other by phone one day, and Rebecca apparently didn't exhibit the "right" amount of enthusiasm for the gift. My mom wasn't offended; she knew her tastes differed from ours. She simply told Rebecca she'd replace the t-shirt with another gift, and she'd keep the t-shirt for herself. But then mom's gears started churning. If Rebecca didn't like her shirt, what about Paula? She popped a letter in the mail making me the same offer.

The day my gift arrived, I immediately called and left my mom a thank you message on her answering machine. The loving words she had written in her card were worth thousands of dollars to me. This was my *experience*. It didn't matter that I rarely wear t-shirts, or that bright yellow is not my best color. I was touched by her thoughtfulness in taking time to send a birthday present while she was on vacation.

The next day, a visiting friend admired the t-shirt, which I'd hung on my closet door. "Do you like it?" I asked. She said "Yes." "Then it's yours." The gift I received and experienced became the gift I gave away.

My mom's letter asking if I liked the t-shirt arrived a few weeks later, telling me to leave her a message if I wanted a different gift. I didn't respond, because I didn't want a different gift. I appreciated the gift, even though it wasn't something I chose to keep.

In the past, I might have kept that t-shirt, switching it dutifully from my dresser to my summer storage and back again, moving it from one house to another. I would have cluttered up my life with it, waiting with bated breath every time I saw my mother for the inevitable question: "Where's the t-shirt I bought you?"

So many times we act, or don't act, because we're afraid of offending others. We tithe, or don't tithe, because we are concerned what others may think. We keep things we *don't* want, or get rid of things we *do* want, because we don't want to cause hurt feelings.

How many things in your home are taking up valuable space and time, because you don't want to hurt someone dear to you? It may be hand-me-down furniture from your parents, kitchen gadgets from your sister, a tacky vase from an aunt, crocheted coasters from your grandmother, a hideous piece of artwork from your boss or co-worker.

It may be something you truly desired at one time, but which has now fulfilled its purpose.

What about the things *you* loved that you got rid of because someone *else* didn't like them? What are you holding on to or letting go of out of *guilt*? Why are you willing to offend your own sensibilities and encroach on your own space or disappoint yourself, but you're not willing to risk offending someone else? It's time to stop feeling guilty about embracing things that resonate with your heart and letting go of things that don't.

You can never truly practice the art of tithing until you're honest with yourself in all your affairs. This is most especially true when you are receiving gifts from others. When you clutter up your life with things you don't truly desire, you leave no room for your true desires to manifest.

Three easy steps can keep you centered on your true desires when you're receiving something.

1. Give thanks for the *intention* of the gift; for the experience of the gift. Assume all gifts are given with lovingkindness and without strings. Other people may have personal reasons for giving you something, and those may appear to be strings attached; in reality we project those strings because we're not allowing the gift to be given freely. We may be so wrapped up in not offending someone that we may *perceive* they are attached to the gift they gave when they're only attached to our happiness.

2. Determine *why* you're holding onto a gift that makes you feel uncomfortable or that you don't like. Examine your motivation thoroughly. Why are you putting someone else's approval of you above your own comfort?

3. Find someone who will appreciate the gift more than you will. Then give them the gift.

A woman I knew perfected this process. I remember visiting her home in New Jersey at Christmas-time one year. She methodically sorted the gifts she had received, showed them off one by one and related a delightful story about the gift giver. Occasionally, she ask if I liked a particular gift. If I answered affirmatively, she said, "Here, it's yours."

She clearly held the gift giver in the highest regard. She appreciated their love and the thoughtfulness of their gift. And she knew she didn't have to hang onto gifts she would not use. No need to feel guilty about passing them along. She was thankful to have experienced the gifts, expressed her thanks and then tithed them to me, while completely immersed in gratitude for the gifts.

Practice the Art of Unconditional Releasing

Your lasting good will never come through forcing personal will.
—Florence Scovel Shinn

You can practice the art of unconditional releasing whenever you tithe, whether you're releasing money, possessions, thoughts or the outcome of an event.

One year, I was putting together birthday presents for a young niece and I was struck by the desire to give her a ceramic beaded figurine her great-grandmother had made for me. I knew in a few years this figurine would have great meaning for her and willingly released it to her.

Jump start the process of getting into the flow of abundance. Look around your house every day for the next 30 days. Select one thing daily that you were given (or purchased) to release. Give thanks for the item, release it, give it a new home (even if it's the local landfill), and sit back and watch what happens. Watch the change in your consciousness, in the way you think and feel. If clutter and debt are both challenges for you, I encourage you to read *Effortless Freedom From Clutter and Debt.*

Every time I systematically give away my treasures, I receive incredible gifts in return. Once, I gave away a whole batch of items I no longer desired to keep. I was immediately rewarded with new prized treasures including a large framed beach picture, a wooden easel, three new sweaters and a new lamp.

Throughout the month, keep a journal to record what you receive as a result of giving freely from your possessions as well as from your time and your abilities. You'll be pleasantly surprised at all the gifts you're already unconsciously experiencing.

Session 5 Questions for Discussion

1. What differences did you notice when you tithed first, before doing anything else with your money? What fears came up? What positive feelings did you experience?

2. Which words do you find most challenging to eliminate from your vocabulary? Which did you find yourself unconsciously using?

3. What happened with the situation you were *seeing* differently?

4. What are you willing, ready and able to do toward your heart's desire? Are there things you think you *should* do or *need to* do? What would happen if you only did things that you truly wanted to do toward your desire?

5. Where have you tithed to feed need in the past? Where have you withheld your tithe, because you didn't *perceive* there was a need? How else has your consciousness changed since you started this course? Where do you find yourself still drawn to feed need?

6. How has your comfort level with tithing changed since you started this course?

7. What are you afraid to pursue for yourself? What price are you willing to pay for what you want?

8. What progress are you and others seeing toward your intentions? Are any revisions needed on any intentions?

Session 5 Activities (do one or more after Session 5)

1. Make a list of everyone you have ever envied, judged, manipulated, shortchanged or given gifts to with attachments. Write a letter of apology to 3-5 people on your list. Apologize for the fear that drove you to that action. If anything needs to be set right, make an offer to correct the situation, even if you have to start small. Mail the letters to each person's last known address. Supercharge your progress by continuing every day to send a letter to someone until you've written everyone on your list.

2. Start a *Progress Report*, writing down each thing you are willing to do toward being, doing or experiencing what you desire in your life. Daily record all progress involving your desire, no matter how small the movement is—even if your initial perception is that it's a step backward. Every day, read through your *Progress Report* to see what movement you've made toward your desire, staying fully focused on

what you want and what has moved you forward; give no thought to what hasn't appeared yet, or reasons why you aren't yet where you want to be.

3. Continue to hold each person's intention in prayer.

4. Ask people to help you tithe of your words by pointing out when you use any of the words or phrases from the *Abundance Zapper* at the back of this book. Use the replacement phrases instead.

5. Use a fresh *Prosperity Tracker* to track the good that comes to you.

Now that you've completed Session 5, begin tithing 5%

Chapter Six

Before Session 6:

• Read Chapter 6

During Session 6:

• Discuss your experience doing
the activities from Chapter 5

• Discuss the questions at the end of this chapter

After Session 6:

• Begin tithing 6%

• Do one or more of the activities listed
at the end of this chapter

Practicing Acts of Courage

Courage is resistance to fear, mastery of fear—
not absence of fear.

—MARK TWAIN

Why is it so hard to practice acts of courage? The fear of not having enough, or missing out, have become ingrained habits.

My friend Barbara works harder than anyone else I know to break this habit. She once went into a restaurant to order dinner. A well-dressed man in the restaurant looked sort of lost, and her first thought was that maybe he was homeless but his clothes made her think otherwise. She struggled internally with offering him some food. Eventually, she walked over and asked him if he would like something to eat. His face lit up with gratitude, and he accepted her offer. So she bought two meals, one for each of them, and gave him dinner. But she did more than that, in truth. She fed his soul. The gratitude in his face fed her soul in return and was something she carried with her for weeks.

I've often struggled with my own intuition, as you probably have also, which says "give that person some money" when they ask (or even when they don't). Then the ego's internal tape recorder clicks on, telling us they'll only use the money for drugs or booze or that the amount of money we have is all we have, and if we give it away then we can't get the chai latte we've been dreaming about all day.

Maybe you have an impulse to give someone a large amount of money. Maybe your tithe that week is larger than usual, or you are moved to tithe more than 10%. Then you begin worrying about how your gift will be perceived. Will it be viewed as charity? Will they think there are strings attached? Then our ego mind goes into full swing: *Are* there strings attached? *Why* do I want to give this money? Should I give it all here, or divide it up into smaller amounts? What if I need this money down the road, if the car breaks down or a client cancels, or I lose my job?

Before you know it, you've talked yourself out of the courageous act of tithing that would have brought you closer to your own innate abundance. The only question you truly need to ask yourself is: What would *Love* do now?

We would all like to practice more generosity and less stinginess. But fear gets in the way. We fear not having enough. We fear needing later what we have now and we fear that when "later" comes we will not have what we need, or that others will not provide. We lack the faith we need to step out of our fear.

I had the perfect opportunity to practice stepping out of my fear when I stopped to pump gas late one winter evening. I had a ten dollar bill and a hundred dollar bill in my wallet. I knew the gas attendant couldn't break a hundred given the late hour, so my intention was to pump $10 worth of gas. As I went inside to prepay, I noticed a bedraggled man standing peacefully in the cold outside the gas station. I instantly thought I should tithe to him, but I realized the only thing I had available to tithe was a hundred dollar bill. *My* hundred dollar bill. Tithing a hundred dollars to a complete stranger seemed insane. I pushed the thought from my head.

I went inside and waited in line to prepay for my gas. The thought jumped into my mind again. I went outside to pump the gas and saw him, still standing there, and the thought came again. I had a complete internal argument about the pros and cons of giving this stranger my hundred dollars while pumping gas. *What if I need this money? What if there was something else I was supposed to do with this money?*

I walked past the man again to get my receipt and immediately knew I would be provided with enough and more than enough, *if* I were willing to give all I had. I decided right then to give the man the $100. I walked outside with my receipt in hand, reaching for my wallet to pull out the $100 bill. The man had disappeared. I looked up and down the street and all around the gas station, but he was gone.

All that had been asked of me was to be *willing* to give; to have the courage to believe my good wasn't tied to that hundred dollar bill.

Our fear is a tricky monkey. It tries convincing us that everything will be okay as long as we have what we have. As long as things don't change.

The truth is: Nothing is going to remain the same simply because we say it should. Not our jobs, relationships, finances—nothing. When things start changing our first impulse is to resist—usually with some sort of aggressive feeling, thought, word or action. We rebel against change and wrap ourselves around that rebellion, until it becomes enmeshed in our lives. Until it *becomes* our lives.

The Venerable Buddhist nun Khandro Rinpoche uses a wonderful example that illustrates how our resistance to change keeps us stuck where we are, struggling against lack and limitation.

She likens life to a pillar with one end of a chain loosely wrapped around it. The other end is not tied to anything. Yet we pick up the end of the chain that looks loose, grasp it tightly and then blame the pillar for us being stuck where we are. We never look to see that we're the ones keeping us chained to an undesirable situation.

The only way to move past thoughts of lack and limitation is to embrace the willingness to let go. You must learn to cultivate courage, to cultivate the knowledge and the faith that abundance will flow in all areas of your life if you are open and receptive to it coming from many different channels.

Cultivating courage is not about fearlessness. Cultivating courage is about having a willingness to stay present even in the face of fear, even in the face of perceived loss. To not run from the hard, scary places in ourselves and in our relationships with others, or in our relationship with money. To not shut down or turn away in frustration, anger or disappointment, but to simply stay the course when you want to flee.

Courage is not about taking a defiant stance or stubbornly pushing your will through, no matter what. Courage is not about demanding a situation go your way.

Courage is about learning to be—to just be—with whatever is occurring in your life, moment by moment.

Embrace Impermanence

A Chinese proverb says water can either float *a ship or sink it. But did you ever notice that it's not the water outside the ship that causes it to sink?*

—JUANITA RUTH ONE

The *only* constant in this world is change. Nothing is permanent. And nothing outside of ourselves will ever give us what we seek. As you move through this book, I hope you begin to realize that all true wealth—every heart's desire you have—is fulfilled as a result of internal changes, your internal transformation.

Lasting wealth comes when you stop grasping at the job or partner or income or other thing *outside yourself* as your source of prosperity. True wealth comes when you stop looking at yourself as being in pain. When you stop looking at something outside yourself as the thing that is causing the pain—or as the only thing that can remove the pain.

Pain comes from a judgment we make about something. Pain comes from a thought or feeling about a situation that occurs. When we become willing to let go of judgment, when we become willing to change our viewpoint and our belief about a situation, pain disappears.

Learn to be more comfortable with impermanence in your life. Impermanence frightens us because we are all control freaks at some core level, and we are all living in a world that cannot be controlled. The good news is there are three areas where you, and you alone, have complete control in your life: *Your thoughts, words and actions.*

You create your life with every thought, word and deed. You, and you alone, can control your thoughts, words and actions. As long as your thoughts, words and deeds come from mistrust, you will not trust the good that appears in your life. You must take on the responsibility for relearning how to trust. *Trust* is the key to tithing from your thoughts, words and actions.

The biblical book of Jeremiah (17:7-8) says, "The person who trusts in the Lord will be blessed. The Lord will show him that he can be trusted. He will be strong, like a tree planted near water that sends its roots by a stream. It is not afraid when the days are hot; its leaves are always green. It does not worry in a year when no rain comes; it always produces fruit."

We all seek a balm to alleviate our fears so we can be more comfortable with the impermanence in our relationships, finances and other areas of our lives. There is no balm. We cannot (and should not) alleviate the fear. That would be like treating the symptoms instead of treating the cause of the dis-ease (discomfort).

Instead, cultivate courage so you can dis-empower the fear. You must face the fear head on. In the movie *The Edge*, Anthony Hopkins and Alec Baldwin are stranded in Alaska with a man-eating Kodiak bear on their trail. The bear represents their fear. They can't outrun it; they can't hide from it. Fear relies on your running and hiding. You feed your fear when you allow yourself to be governed by the voices that say giving back a tenth of what you have been given will leave you with *not enough*.

Face your fears head-on and catch it off guard. Once off guard, fear is immediately diminished. It's dis-empowered and can be conquered. Tithing in all areas of your life is the most effective way to face your fears head-on. Each time you tithe and a fear rises up, you are gifted with an opportunity to recognize the fear, face it and disempower it.

When you tithe, and a worry or fear comes to mind, remind yourself you have three choices:

1. **Stay with the suffering and feed the fear.** You can let the fear eat you up by withholding your tithe, or by giving your tithe while simultaneously holding onto the fear that by tithing you are giving away some-

thing you need, making a mistake or causing your-self to not have *enough* later.

2. **Do something that causes the fear to be masked, so you don't experience it now.** This is a popular way of running away from the fear. You can repeat affirmations or deny the fear, trying to convince yourself that the fear is not real or warranted.

3. **Stay present.** Acknowledge the strength of the fear, face it head on and convert your fear into an impetus for action. Focus on your heart's desire and all the good in your life. Recognize all the ways—large and small—that giving has resulted in you receiving even greater good in other areas of your life. Allow your fear to feed your courage. Allow your fear to feed your soul.

The best way to measure how in touch you are with your inherent, prosperous self is to ask yourself how well you are able to practice non-grasping. It's like Dorothy in *The Wizard of Oz*, repeating *"Lions and tigers and bears, oh, my!"* as she continued down the yellow brick road.

How well are you able to let go and take action, facing your fear head on? Giving thanks feeds your soul as much as it feeds the soul of those who receive your gifts.

Worried about the current state of your finances, health, relationships or other areas of your life? Ask the Universe for simple reminders that your systematic giving has awakened your awareness to the Divine Flow. Even little, everyday reminders can help you stay focused on your dream life. Ask God to send you a sign of your innate abundance every day, but especially anytime your chest tightens over an issue.

The signs may be as simple as a penny on the sidewalk or a note or gift from someone who expresses their thanks for you being in their life or for doing the work you do. Be receptive to these little reminders that you already have everything you need today. Sometimes, all we need is a reminder that our futures are as bright as a newly minted penny.

Project an Aura of Abundance

"Every man can multiply his own ability by almost constant wordless realization of his unity with his Source."

—WALTER RUSSELL

An old adage from twelve-step programs says, *Act as If*. Act as if you're financially secure, and the peace of financial security will be yours. Act as if you are confident in your abilities, and you will be able to achieve countless things. Act as if you are unafraid in a relationship, and you will find the courage to take the next step in that relationship. Act as if you understand how to handle money, and you will discover the information you need to be more comfortable about handling your finances. Act as if you are vibrant, energized and healthy and you will begin to feel more vibrant and energetic. Act as if you believe you have enough money to share and enough to spare and you always will.

A man's jaw literally dropped when he learned a certain woman had grown up in modest circumstances. He was surprised to hear this because she actually exudes affluence. Everything about her, including the way she carries herself and her self-confidence, made him feel certain she had grown up wealthy. She believed his perception was a direct result of her growing prosperity consciousness.

The words we speak, the clothes we wear, and the sturdiness of our posture all reflect our thoughts about ourselves and our abundance.

Do you whine about how hard your luck has been recently, how bad you are feeling these days, how awful your relationship is, how poor the economy is? Or do you point out how you feel something big is just around the corner, how you're feeling more healthy than the day before, how sweet your spouse was in some way, how business is looking up these days, how your income is growing every day, in every way?

Do you wear rag-tag, sloppy clothes, or do you crisply iron even your most threadbare t-shirt so you present an image of someone who cares about the life you've created for yourself so far? Do you slouch when you stand, giving the impression of someone who is beaten and victimized, or do you stand tall, expectant and grateful? Do you engage in sarcasm and gossip and encourage others to be righteously indignant or do you speak kind words, point out someone's good qualities and encourage people to work out their differences? Changing your inner and outer appearances are small changes you can make in your everyday life to tip the scales toward abundance.

While on a business trip to Chicago, I once had the good fortune of meeting a highly-motivated young woman named Cathleen Carr. At the time, Cathleen was a struggling actor. Today, she's a well-known actor, writer and producer in New York. With a little downtime on my hands I was looking for something to read, and Cathleen reached into her bag and presented me with a dog-eared copy of *The Tipping Point* by Malcolm Gladwell. Although she'd long ago finished the book she carried it around with her for inspiration. After reading it from cover to cover in less than 48 hours, I could see why.

Gladwell believed that little changes could make a huge difference in our world. He looked at how epidemics (anything that has gained momentum and created exponential growth) have been tipped, or reached critical mass, simply by tinkering with the smallest details of the immediate environment. For instance, let's look at what caused New York City's murder rate to plummet in the mid-1990s.

It all started when New York City's new transit authority director shared his thoughts about how to create fundamental changes in people's beliefs and behavior on the subway system. He believed changes would persist and serve as examples to others if he created a community for new beliefs to be practiced, expressed and nurtured.

Following this theory, he began cracking down on the area where subway riders were being visually assaulted: subway graffiti. Under the new transit policy, no subway car would leave the train yard with graffiti. Next, he began targeting fare-beaters. He assumed the more often people saw others jumping turnstiles, the more likely they would decide they shouldn't have to pay either. Catching and chaining fare-beaters to the turnstile gates, his subway officers sent a message that lawlessness would not be allowed. Housewives, gang members and business executives all received the same treatment. No major changes were made in the way New York City police officers carried out their other duties or how they pursued other crimes.

Even so, both violent and petty crime plummeted and continued to be lower than crime in many other cities. The tipping point for reducing the murder rate and increasing law and order in New York City resulted from eliminating everyday signs of disorder in the subway system like graffiti, fare-beating and broken windows.

What broken windows, graffiti and other signs of disorder in your world invite poverty, lack and limitation into your life? Can the tipping point for reducing your difficulties and increasing your earning power, your satisfaction in relationships, your level of health and your abundance in all other areas be as simple and as trivial as repairing broken windows, eliminating graffiti and cracking down on fare-beaters? Can the tipping point for creating global prosperity be just as simple? After careful reflection, I decided it may be true.

Where are your broken windows? Where is your view distorted by old beliefs? Where are you acting impoverished instead of embracing the good that exists in your relationships, your financial affairs, your health and every other area of your life? Some of the most beautiful windows in the world are made of broken glass: stained-glass windows.

Where are you seeing or adding to the graffiti in your life? Graffiti can be verbal as well as visual. Your words carry immense power. Your words can tear someone down or build someone up. Your words can either defeat you or empower you.

You can eliminate the graffiti in your life by refusing to engage in gossip, refusing to take part in negative conversations about people and events (including yourself!), and by consciously choosing to affirm the abundance in all things. Make a declaration of your independence from the economy. Declare that talk about recession, unemployment, inflation, lack, poverty and debt have no power over you, any more than King George had power over American colonists.

Where are you engaging in fare-beating? Where are you trying to get something for nothing? Where are you trying to beat the system, being dishonest in your interactions with yourself or others? Are you surreptitiously taking time away from your employer or not working at your fullest potential, padding a bill to a customer, or withholding information from loved ones in order to avoid their hurt, disappointment or anger? Or maybe you're complaining about never getting a break while at the same time never giving others a break, or never giving thanks for what you already have, by giving a portion of it back to the Source where it came from?

A few simple changes in your outer circumstances can easily raise your inner vibration. Once your senses perceive that signs of lack and limitation are being reduced, it becomes easier to see the limitless good in your life. Ready to create a positive epidemic of prosperity in your life?

Start by being up front and honest about what you need and expect. The results may surprise you. Whenever you catch yourself saying or thinking, "I know I shouldn't, but . . ." or, "I know I should, but . . . ," stop and reconsider. Then consciously choose to either continue in the direction you were heading with your thoughts, words and actions, or consciously choose to move forward in a new, more positive direction.

Choose to speak right words. *Choose* to think right thoughts. *Choose* to see things rightly—from a perception of *Love*. *Choose* to take right action. *Choose* to give thanks with all your words, thoughts and actions. *Choose* to bring your full tithe to your spiritual Source as an offering of your gratitude and thanks.

You cannot truly tithe of your material good while withholding the tithe of your spirit. Do not withhold justice, mercy, kindness, love. Turn every thought, word and deed into a selfless tithe. You are the only one who can control your thoughts, words and deeds. You are the only one who has the power to choose something different.

Session 6 Questions for Discussion

1. What was the hardest part of writing and sending the letters from last session? What changes in yourself and others did you observe after you sent the letters? If you haven't sent the letters, what are you afraid will happen if you do? What's your payoff for *not* sending the letters?

2. What fears have been holding you back from doing what it is you truly desire to do, especially regarding sharing your innate gifts with others? How have you chosen to let these fears hold you back from living a fully prosperous life, with what you have today?

3. Given the current state of your finances, what things can you begin to do *today* to fully enjoy your current life? What if today is the day you get to do the things you've always wanted to do, and nothing outward had to change in *your* finances? What would you do *today* if fear got out of the way?

4. How has your definition of abundance changed since you began this course? In what new ways have you begun to embrace your abundance? What emotional struggles around financial issues have you given up since you started this course?

5. What attachments do you have to *your money*? What would happen if you began to view everything as omnipresent, omnipotent Divine Universal Energy, instead of with a more limited view of something being *yours*, *mine* or *theirs*?

6. How can you make sure you're putting Divine Love first, rather than ego, when you tithe?

7. What actions have you taken to bless and prosper others since you started this program? How has your gratitude and generosity returned to you?

8. In the past, when you've tithed, *how* have you tithed? What has been your state of mind when you gave your tithe? How is that different today?

9. What words do you usually say when you receive something? If you're not sure, ask your friends and family—they'll be glad to tell you what your usual response is!

10. What abundant gifts have you received recently that you had been overlooking? What offered gifts are you the steward of right now?

11. What things are you holding onto that make you feel uncomfortable, or that you don't like? Why are you holding onto these things?

Session 6 Activities (do one or more after Session 6)

1. Make a list of who you feel "owes you" financially, emotionally, with their time, etc. Reaffirm the trust you placed in that person. Set an intention for them that they are growing more and more aware of their true nature as Abundance. Write a letter to 3-5 people you feel *owe* you and let them know you are forgiving the debt, consider it a gift, and no longer feel they owe you anything. Apologize for making people indebted to you emotionally or time-wise. Send letters to the last known address for each person. Release your attachment to the debt and make room for this good to appear in another form, from another channel.

2. Keep track of all the channels through which abundance flows through you. Make a two-column list: *Tithes From Others* and *Tithes To Others*. List the many non-monetary ways people tithed to you recently. List all the non-monetary ways you have tithed to others (Words, Actions, Thoughts, Possessions, Abilities, Time).

3. Create a gift recording journal. Assign a monetary value to everything you receive this week. Include intangibles (confirmation you're on the right track) as well as tangibles.

4. Make a list of all items taking up space in your home; things you no longer want, need or desire. Give something away to someone every day this week. Give thanks for the item, release it and give it a new home (even if that new home is the local landfill).

5. Continue holding each person's intention in prayer.

6. Continue watching the words you say.

7. Use a fresh *Prosperity Tracker* to track the good that comes to you this week.

Now that you've completed Session 6, begin tithing 6%

Chapter Seven

Before Session 7:
- Read Chapter 7

During Session 7:
- Discuss your experience doing the activities from Chapter 6
- Discuss the questions at the end of this chapter

After Session 7:
- Begin tithing 7%
- Do one or more of the activities listed at the end of this chapter

Setting Your Intentions

How do you spend most of your time:
worrying or trusting?
Trust is expecting the best to happen.
Worry is expecting the worst to happen.
What did you really expect would happen?

Every August, just before my birthday, I set my intentions for what I want to receive in the coming year. So often, we set our intention about what we want, and then we focus our energy on the fact that we haven't yet received it. In August of 2001, I set my intention and expressed my desire to receive $4,000 in cash, gifts or ideas, every day. I determined that I would consciously focus my attention on *where* I was receiving this $4,000 rather than on how much actual money I was receiving.

I allowed myself to be *worth* $4,000 a day. I chose to receive the $4,000 and let go of any expectation of how those results would be achieved. I lived each day with a sense of eager anticipation. Like an expectant mother I did not wonder *if* I would give birth; I merely wondered *how and in what form* the new blessing would appear.

When people donated their time to watch my dog, gave me a massage, took me out to dinner, gave me books, spent time sharing ideas, I valued those things. Not only did I value them, I placed a value upon them and I recorded that amount.

I did the same for ideas that were sparked by circumstances. Something I read, something I heard, something divinely passed along to me in meditation. Everything received a value: What could this idea be worth to me?

I placed the value on the idea and then immediately took action to follow up (thus putting into motion the energy needed to make that value manifest). When I had a workshop idea for a particular audience, I wrote to the person in charge. When I had a theological idea, I asked questions to guide my search and followed where the answers led. And so on.

I actively saw cash manifesting as well. I did not see $4,000 a day in cash, but my actual business income exceeded monthly projections, and my personal income rose as well. It all changed because—rather than creating *expectations*—I created an *expectancy*.

Your desires manifest when you change your attitude—your expectations—to reflect your true self-worth. Your desires manifest when you look for, see and acknowledge the many different forms abundance takes in your life. Let go of your expectations and replace them with a new-found expectancy. Replace your expectations with *anticipations*. Expectancy is about anticipation. Expectancy transports you from a mindset that wonders "Will I get what I want?" to a mindset that wonders "In what exciting way will what I want come into my life?"

Expectancy incorporates a knowingness. Know that what you desire is enroute and anticipate its arrival with great joy. For 30 days, replace your expectations with anticipations and you will immediately begin to see results in your life.

I first shared this technique with my son when he was five years old, impatiently waiting for food to be served at restaurants. As most of us do when hungry, he constantly focused on "when is our food going to be here? What's taking so long?" We taught him to realize it was already here, by stating "It's here!" At first his ego would fight this concept, spreading his hands across the table to demonstrate that it was indeed *not* "here." Or he would say "It's here!" with the wishful expectation that it would now magically appear where it was not. The minute he would truly surrender and say "It's here!" and mean it? He would turn his head and the table would be overflowing with an abundance of food. He tithed of his thoughts and was well-rewarded.

So many other stories demonstrate this principle. A woman tithed at my seminar, and set her intention to have the right and perfect job that would feed her soul and provide her with the income she desired. Within thirty days she had manifested not one but *two* job offers that exactly matched what she'd declared.

Another woman manifested an unexpected $9,000 24 hours after aligning her attitude with thanksgiving.

A third woman tithed $41 at my workshop. Two days later she received a bonus from her job in the amount of $3,900. She had never received a bonus this large in the past. She attributes it to her tithe, since the amount received was nearly 100 times what she'd tithed—which is what she set her intention to receive!

Align Your Actions With Your Intentions

Many people use their money with right intention, giving to support causes they care about, even though they do not tithe. Remember: You have no *obligation* to tithe. You have an *opportunity* to tithe. You may be perfectly satisfied with all areas of your life and you may see no need to tithe. Spending your money with right intention may be enough for you.

For example, you may buy organic food or from local farms, to support your commitment to environmental values and local producers. You may buy fair trade items to support developing countries or you may buy secondhand to support recycling. You may make financial donations to organizations you support.

Supporting your commitment to your values is a very sound approach to giving. This strategy will draw to you the same energy you extend. You attract like-minded people, and strengthen your values in these areas. Would you like to provide even greater support to these worthy causes? If so, tithing is the best way I know to increase your abundance so you have more to share with these worthy causes.

Remember: Tithing is a form of intentional giving. By tithing, you give back to the Universe a portion of what the Universe has given you as a way of saying "Thank you for supporting me in my ventures here on this planet."

Helping support the planet through your purchases is noble and worthy, *and* it is important to offer the same support to your spiritual Source—in whatever form Spirit moves you—so the planet continues to thrive. For instance, you support a particular artist when you buy their painting or a ticket to their concert. This is not a tithe. This is a gift. However, if you send additional money to that artist, because a song or a piece of art really touched your spirit and fed your soul, *that* amount would be a tithe. A tithe is a gift of thanksgiving, with no expectation of anything in return. Allow your conscience to be your guide. When you tithe, you're giving to express your thanks for something that fed your spirit with no expectation of anything in return.

Your spiritual Source will appear through illimitable channels in your life, just as your good, your abundance, will appear through those same endless channels. Your tithing consciousness will evolve over time, so be patient with the process.

When I first started tithing, I sent money to causes I believed in that helped children, particularly abused children and children who were runaways or throw-aways. Even as I gave, I could sense something was missing. So I started tithing to spiritual organizations I knew were open and receptive to universal approaches to Spirit (such as the local Unitarian-Universalist and Unity churches), even though I had never attended them or been spiritually fed by them.

Once I started really *getting* the premise of tithing—giving back a portion of my good to the spiritual Source from which it came—I started giving to various channels that fed my spirit each week. I would observe where my soul leaped up and sang for joy because of an encounter with someone, something I read, something I heard, something I saw. I would tithe to those people and places immediately. These inspirations helped me learn more about myself and my spirituality.

I've tithed to churches where I've spoken, to waiters whose incredible late night service nearly brought me to tears, and to hotel housekeeping staff for joyously giving me room to work. I've tithed directly to ministers, friends, homeless people, children and so on. I've tithed to organizations that help impoverished children and support global peace efforts.

When you step out in faith and tithe a full 10% of your income with gratitude, incredible things occur. Good appears everywhere in your life, and you can give even more to organizations you cherish. I now give much more to charities from my increased income, above and beyond the 10% that I give as a *thank you* for my daily soul food.

As I said before, your tithing consciousness will evolve over time. Only you can determine where you're comfortable tithing. Concerned, worried or uncomfortable with where you're tithing? I recommend engaging in my *Conscious Tithing* exercise for ninety days and tap into the true power of tithing.

Here's how *Conscious Tithing* works. Mark off ninety days on the calendar. During those ninety days, practice the art of tithing by giving away 10% of whatever income you receive each day—with immense gratitude—to someone who feeds your spirit. It could be a homeless man on the corner who suddenly lifts you out of a blue mood, because you realize how insignificant your problems are compared to his today. It could be a child whose innocence brings a smile to your face. It could be a writer who brings you an "Aha!" moment with his writing. It could be a musician whose song helps you heal. It could be a waitress whose kind demeanor brightens your day. It could be an organization whose commitment to their cause gives you hope for the future of humanity. It could be a minister or a church, a speaker or writer, whose spiritual message gives you the strength you need to do what you think you cannot.

Do not prejudge who you're tithing to or where you're tithing. Do not use your tithe to *feed need.* Do not withhold your tithe from one place thinking they don't have a need for it. Wherever your spirit is fed, to whomever feeds your soul, tithe.

Take the income you receive that day (or the day before, which is easier to do since you already know how much that was!) and give away 10% of it, on the spot.

Tithe the 10% and give thanks for the blessings in your life. The day you start your ninety days, write down your current income, your current financial situation and net worth—and how you feel about all three.

Record the gifts and blessings you receive daily; the things you're grateful for, and the income and unexpected gifts (tangible and intangible) that come to you. In addition, during those ninety days, write down your thoughts and feelings about tithing.

At the end of the ninety days, check to see what has changed in your finances, in the other areas of your life, and in the way you think and feel about tithing. I know you'll be pleasantly surprised.

A woman I met in Arizona was worried about being able to sell her home quickly. She tithed and set her intention to sell her home, at the right and perfect price to the right and perfect people, within thirty days. She began taking action as she was guided. She started by cleaning out the house. Then she determined what she wanted to do to get the house ready for sale. Everything she asked for came effortlessly, even things that had proved difficult in the past. She declared the house would find its new owners. Her Realtor said the strangest thing happened when the new owners were first shown the house. The wife felt she just had to have that very house. None other would do.

What major goal have you been trying to accomplish? Set your intention today and start tithing to give thanks for the good that already exists in your life, then take steps to bring you toward your goal. I guarantee you'll accomplish your goal before you know it.

A man knew tithing worked, but for several months he resisted giving thanks and had (according to him!) become downright lazy in sending his tithes to his spiritual organization. He eventually sent a check and a month later received a pay raise.

He began to tithe 10% of whatever cash he had at the end of the day, depositing it in the ATM of the local bank, so he could write out a monthly check to his spiritual organization. The very next day, he received another check from his employer giving him another substantial monthly raise. His part-time Reiki practice also began taking off.

Setting your intention to tithe is a powerful step. Greater good will appear in your life even before you begin to send out your tithe. Be very cautious, however, if you decide to save up your tithes in order to give *monthly*, as this man did. It's very easy for our egos to get in the way and look at the money we've set aside and decide, "Oh, it's not quite enough yet to tithe." or "This is far too much to tithe!" or "I'll tithe part now and save the rest in case I need it later."

I once gave guidance to a salesman who was a first time tither. His faith was immediately rewarded when he began to tithe. He had the best sales week he'd ever had, even though sales were down for everyone else in the company. His commission check was over $4,000, and his boss told him he wanted to talk with him about a promotion. Everything he touched seemed to turn to gold.

When he sat down to tithe the next month, he realized his tithe check would be over $400. His ego began wondering what else he could be doing with that $400. He decided to use the money to pay bills instead.

Suddenly, his income stream dried up. Clients were hesitant to buy. His boss kept delaying their scheduled meeting regarding his promotion.

He called me in a panic. He realized he had withheld his tithe, and now he no longer had $400 to tithe. What did he have an abundance of? Self-help books! I recommended he tithe $400 worth of books to a men's shelter or other organization helping people get on their feet. Once he pulled those books off his bookshelves and delivered them, the abundance in his life began to effortlessly flow again.

Release Control

To have and not to give is often worse than to steal.

—MARIE VON EBNER-ESCHENBACH

We all like feeling we individually control our destiny. Because of this, when things start going well, we tell the Universe, "Okay, thanks for the directions. I'll take over from here." Then, as conductors of our own life's train, we stop listening as that Still Small Voice Within tries to tell us, "Hey, you, wake up! The bridge up ahead is out." We're so busy explaining to that Infinite Intelligence how "we've got everything under control!" that we overlook the warning signs and signals the Universe sends our way, including the helping hands pointing us in the right direction.

When things are going well, we feel in control. Then, as things start to get out of control and fall apart, our thoughts, words and actions suddenly shift. We begin to get frustrated. We begin focusing our attention on the problem instead of on what we desire. We start blaming others, trying to fix the problem by ourselves and forgetting we had help pulling it all together.

How to keep from getting off track? How to get back on track if your attitude of thanksgiving becomes derailed? Mentally relive your day and count your blessings as you're nodding off to sleep. "Count your many blessings, name them one by one" as the children's song says. Let your last thoughts every day be filled with gratitude for all the ways Spirit moved in your life that day. And focus your first thoughts in the morning on gratitude for how Spirit *will* move during the newly dawned.

Here's one daily practice I highly recommend doing— either at the end of the day or the very beginning. Write down ordinary things you are grateful for—things we might generally take for granted. Like central heating, indoor plumbing, toilet paper, a bed, clean water and so on. Remembered blessings increases gratitude.

A woman practiced the art of tithing faithfully for quite some time and saw it working in her life. Then she started calling it success and thought she was responsible for what she had and for creating more. The further she strayed from abundant thinking and gratitude for her bounty, the more complicated her life became, even though she continued to tithe.

Eventually she completely forgot she was abundant, until one day she realized what she was doing to herself and her family. She looked around at the gifts in her life and took time to appreciate and enjoy them. She saw with wonderment and surprise that she had a beautiful life and a beautiful family. She had forgotten how truly blessed she was.

Moving her mind back to actively practicing gratitude and abundance, she has experienced positive changes. She considers it a gift from the Universe that—once she recognized the part she played in ejecting abundance and gratitude from her life—reminders and quiet lessons have dropped into her lap from everywhere, gently guiding her back on the path.

A spiritual leader related a story of two people who wanted the last space at a seminar. One person had financial means and was trying to bargain, wanting to pay $500, a sizable discount on the seminar cost. The second person only had $20 and was willing to give it all. When asked who he chose, the speaker replied, "The one who was willing to give everything he had." Where are your thoughts focused? Are your thoughts focused on *getting* as much as you can, or on *giving* as much as you can?

You will always get whatever you are willing to give. *A Course in Miracles* says, "To have all, give all, to all." You cannot expect to get more unless you're first willing to give more. For example, you cannot expect to get better service from someone unless you are willing to give better service as a customer. Remember: tithing involves our thoughts, words *and* actions. We cannot expect to have greater joy in our lives if we aren't first willing to tithe with our thoughts and words as willingly and cheerfully as we tithe with our actions.

One day, I stopped to pump gas while on a long road trip. The machine wouldn't respond properly to my request to pay inside, so I pressed the button for assistance. I could see the two employees inside, chatting and laughing, but the machine continued to say "please wait" and no assistance came. I could feel myself getting frustrated. I was tired and still had hours to drive.

Finally, a clerk stuck her head out the door and asked if I wanted to pay with cash. I stopped myself from being surly and simply said "Yes, but the machine isn't responding." She walked over, mashed two buttons and then turned to me and smiled. She apologized for the problem, and authentically wished for me to have a great day. My ego instantly deflated. I was grateful I hadn't snapped at her for my assumption that she didn't care about me, her customer.

I wanted to be recognized as a valued customer. When I made the assumption I wasn't being valued I withheld the tithe of my spirit, the tithe of my thoughts, and had rude thoughts instead. I recognized the thoughts and chose to make my actions kinder and more compassionate. Because I valued the clerk with my actions, she in turn valued me with her words and actions.

Too often our egos get involved in our giving. Our giving becomes a source of personal recognition instead of pure giving to say *thank you*. If you notice the flow of your good appears blocked, begin practicing the *Conscious Tithing* exercise in every way you tithe. Check your ego if it's getting involved in your tithing efforts. Take steps to release the withheld money, and any resentment or need for recognition as soon as possible.

I once counseled a woman who worked in real estate. She practiced affirmations regularly and had seen them work countless times in the past, yet the flow of prosperity in her life had become stagnant. She began being more conscious with her tithes. She released unwanted treasures and forgave a $4,000 debt to her brother, but she was still unable to move forward financially.

Before she met with me, she took the matter into reflection and realized that when she met her husband, her business took off like crazy, and she was surrounded with positive energy. This all changed after she moved into his home; the woman's business went downhill. During her reflection, her stepdaughter, with whom she had an antagonistic relationship, instantly came to mind.

The woman began saying affirmations that would free her from her stepdaughter's presence. The affirmations, though filled with words of release, were also filled with resentment. Every time she practiced her affirmations, her stepdaughter would stop coming to her home and the woman's business picked up. Eventually, her stepdaughter stopped coming over permanently. When this happened, rather than her business skyrocketing, her business dried up completely.

She continued saying business-building affirmations. Each affirmation was said with feeling and ended with the woman claiming her good and thanking the Universe, yet she still felt stuck. She hadn't released the resentment and therefore never truly gave her tithe with thanksgiving. Once this was pointed out, she revised her affirmations in ways that were loving. She blessed her stepdaughter. Almost immediately, harmony was restored in both her business and home life.

Disharmony in your home or family can cause the flow of good in your life to dwindle. If you find any disharmony in your life, open up the channels of communication in the situation. Recognize the fullness of the peace available to you. Uncover any energy still swirling around you in regard to the disharmony. You may find deep-seated but unspoken anger, fear, resentment or sadness exists where love should exist instead.

We so often want people to change their behavior. We want people to stop doing something, or start doing something, so we will feel better. The truth is, you can never change someone else's behavior. You can, however, change your own behavior and thoughts. Honor yourself and forgive yourself for thinking unkindly of others. Claim responsibility for and acknowledge your role in all disharmony. Then release the situation to its highest good for all concerned.

Here's an excellent forgiveness affirmation: *I forgive and am forgiven for all past thoughts, words and deeds in this situation and I bless and support everyone involved in all their power and magnificence. Thank you, God!*

Find the Freedom in Forgiveness

Human freedom involves our capacity to pause, to choose the one response toward which we wish to throw our weight.

—Marie von Ebner-Eschenbach

A woman once contacted me because she kept receiving tithes of $77. She wondered if there was some significance to the figure. Metaphysically, the number seven represents fullness and perfection. We have the seven wonders of the world, the seven chakras, the seven senses (sight, sound, taste, smell, touch, intuition and telepathy). Seventy times seven carries even more power. This is the number that implies unlimited forgiveness, about which Jesus spoke. A vital step toward creating a life of abundance is mastering the art of forgiveness.

Give forth love and gratitude for every event in your life. See how each experience could be for your highest good. This is true forgiveness.

Whenever you are feeling stuck, look for the bottle-neck of what has yet to be forgiven. The places where you still think someone did something harmful to you. The truth is, everything in all our lives has unfolded for our highest good *and* for the highest good of everyone involved. Our ego does *not* like to admit this. Our ego wants someone else to be *wrong* so we can be *right*. Our ego wants us to be a victim, powerless. Our ego will even try and convince us we've already forgiven *that person*. We *forgive but don't forget*, which is really *not* forgiving. What is unforgiven is transformed into resentments we carry around or gloss over.

You may find the unforgiven lurking in the corner, with a cover draped over it, ever hopeful that keeping it out of sight will keep it out of mind. You may find disharmony hidden away behind a big red brick wall you've built to protect yourself from the pain of dealing with the issue. You cannot push away disharmony, or put it out of sight. It takes more energy to keep disharmony covered up than it does to heal it.

Take a giant leap in your imagination and forgive yourself for *ever* thinking anyone could harm you in any way. The door to your creative consciousness will open wider than ever before.

A woman who had a lifelong dream was frustrated. She felt all her attempts to fulfill her dream had been stymied for more than a decade by people who were jealous of her talents—and by events she took as personal rejection. I had her make a list of everyone she felt had ever held her back professionally. She meticulously listed everyone. Then she imagined that everything she had misperceived as *harmful* had actually been divinely guided for her highest good. She then listed *why* she was thankful for that person or situation—what she had learned and what gifts she had gained from each experience or encounter.

One by one, she released her resentments, thanking everyone for their contributions—which had brought her professionally to where she was at this moment. Six months after forgiving and releasing her resentments, she was well on her way to fulfilling her lifelong dream!

How many times shall you forgive someone? According to the biblical story (Matthew 18:22), true forgiveness comes when you forgive someone *seventy times seven times*, meaning: when you forgive someone abundantly. Forgiveness is simpler than we often make it out to be.

Forgiving someone means making a conscious choice to let go of the story, to let go of the need to be right, to release your ill thoughts of another, and to allow that person to heal and to be happy instead.

Forgiving yourself is equally important. Call to mind every event where you feel you made a mistake. State aloud: "It seemed like a good idea at the time." If it hadn't seemed like a good idea at that moment—for whatever reason—you wouldn't have chosen to do it, right?

Forgiveness is an act of consciously seeing everyone (including yourself!) blessed for their highest good in whatever situation is grieving you. Embrace the number seven and the principle of forgiveness, repeatedly giving forth good thoughts toward others until you are both freed from past stories and resentments. The powerful impact on your life cannot be underestimated.

To restore the flow of harmony and abundance in any area of your life, you must empower yourself. The quickest way to empowerment is to claim responsibility for your role and give forth love to all involved, including yourself. Do you ever wait for someone else to apologize first, even though you have the desire to apologize? When you do this, you're withholding the tithe of your words. Somehow you fear you will lose respect, lose face or lose power in the situation. Give first, with the knowledge that nothing can ever be lost; it can only be converted.

A man was attending church one Sunday when a modern-day prophet stood up to deliver a message, saying God told him to tell whomever was in turmoil about a $20,000 debt that the debt had been forgiven. The man who had carried the indebtedness stood up, crying. The $20,000 was the amount of his unpaid tithes.

Anytime you feel anxious about the flow of abundance in your life, check in with yourself. Ask: "Do I have enough for today?" Not for what you need tomorrow, or the next day, or for what is due next week or next month. Do you have enough for *today*? The truth is you do, even if it means releasing your attachment to what you thought the day was going to look like and what you are attached to doing or having that day. As *A Course in Miracles* so aptly states early on: "Nothing real can be threatened. Nothing unreal exists. Herein lies the peace of God."

If you *lose* something, it wasn't real. It wasn't really for your highest good. It was something outside of yourself your ego wanted to use to make you feel secure, complete or worthy.

Use a reminder affirmation to keep your thoughts focused on the truth about the limitless abundance in your life. One helpful affirmation I recommend: *I already have enough time, energy, wisdom, love and money to accomplish all that I need to accomplish today, Thank You, God!* The best affirmations always begin or end with the words *Thank you, God,* or some other gratitude that acknowledges your Oneness with Universal Flow.

When you find yourself speaking words of limitation, convincing yourself you live paycheck to paycheck, or your relationship can't be salvaged, or the health and energy you have right now is going to run out, use an affirmation to stop your thoughts from drifting away from your connection to abundance.

Use simple affirmations:

What God has given, cannot be diminished.
This is all for my highest good.
Everything is unfolding in Divine Order, in Divine Timing.
All is well.
I am safe and I am loved.

Your ego get a kick out of "messing with you" as my son likes to say. You're the one who has the power and the ability to control your thoughts. Take whatever actions necessary to keep yourself firmly planted in the awareness that you already have everything.

Let me share one last story with you in this chapter. A woman I knew well was to receive an inheritance of $40,000 a year, which would come from a trust fund administered by her and two other trustees. Because she did not have complete control over how the funds would be dispersed to her, she feared not having what she wanted when she needed it. Without complete control over how her inheritance would be paid, she did something amazing.

She refused the inheritance.

Imagine yourself in that situation. Would *you* turn down your inheritance?

If not, then why do you turn down your Divine Inheritance? Become open and receptive to receiving the unlimited abundance that exists in your life today. Establish a firm practice of tithing so you are already giving thanks for the manifestation of your divine inheritance. Then release your expectations of how your inheritance will appear.

Remember: You set your intentions with your thoughts and words, as well as with your deeds. Set your intention to embrace your Divine Inheritance right here, right now.

Session 7 Questions for Discussion

1. How do you feel about the forgiveness work you did? What unexpected awareness of abundance did you receive after you forgave people their debts?
2. What non-monetary ways did other people tithe to you? What non-monetary ways have you tithe to other people?
3. How did it feel to assign a "value" to friendly acts from others, divine ideas or avoided dangers?

4. How does your space feel, since you began giving things away?

5. When faced with a fear this week (even the fear of a perceived loss), what do you think would happen if you stayed present and took a step toward what you desire, rather than shutting down or sabotaging yourself?

6. Since starting this course, how have you consciously turned your thoughts, words and actions toward your good? What new perceptions do you have of how good comes to you emotionally, physically and spiritually? Did any good come to you in unexpected ways? How did you feel when that happened?

7. What persistent reminder can you place in your consciousness to help you stay focused on seeing, blessing and multiplying all that is in your life? What will serve as a reminder that you are Abundance; that you are a blessing in the lives of all you meet? It could be something you say, see or hear.

8. What immediate change are you willing to make in your attitude, words and environment to exude affluence and raise your awareness of your true abundant nature? In what ways can you create or enhance a community where your new beliefs can be practiced, expressed and nurtured?

9. What are the broken windows, graffiti, "fare jump- ers" and other signs of disorder in your life that lead you to perceive poverty, lack and limitation? Where are you seeing or adding to the broken windows, graffiti, fare jumpers and disorder in your life?

10. Where is your view distorted by old beliefs? Where are you acting impoverished instead of perceiving and embracing the abundance that exists in your relationships, your financial affairs, your health and every other area of your life?

11. Where are you trying to get something for noth- ing? Where are you trying to beat the system, not being honest in your interactions with yourself or others? When you're tempted to take a shortcut or shortchange yourself, where are you willing to con- sciously step up and ask for what you truly desire, speak your truth, be authentic?

Session 7 Activities (do one or more after Session 7)

1. Select a "prosperity symbol" for your life. It could be something simple, like raspberries, sunflow- ers, frogs, pumpkins, red cowboy boots, and so on. Something that will make you smile, pause and remember who you are: Divine Love.

2. Make a list of things you feel you "cannot afford" to do. The only thing you cannot afford to do is live

your life with a mindset that supports you having less than the Powerful, Prosperous, Passionate life of your dreams. Look at each item on your list and ask: Do I value myself enough to take the steps necessary to begin to perceive this in my life? Can I let go of my attachment to being in charge of *how* this good is appearing in my life today?

3. Starting this session, begin to set aside an additional 1% of your income into savings, even if it's a jar. On the jar, put a picture of something you desire to be, do or experience.

4. Make a list of any financial debts. Include who you owe and how much you owe. Put each creditor's address on the list. Once a month, send each creditor $1 toward your outstanding balance. The amount you send doesn't matter as much as setting the process into motion. Pay something toward each debt, even if the balances keep going up. *[Editor's Note: If you have not paid on a debt in more than four years, please contact Paula Langguth Ryan before you make a payment on a debt. With some debts, it may not be in your best interest to pay the creditor or collection agency, from a credit reporting standpoint. Actual settlement or repayment of your debt in another way may be a better financial choice.]*

5. Between now and Session 8, look for at least three opportunities to build someone up and empower them, including yourself.

6. Continue your gift recording journal, assigning a monetary value to everything you receive.

7. Continue giving something away to someone every day.

8. Continue holding each person's intention in prayer.

9. Continue watching the words you say.

10. Use a fresh *Prosperity Tracker* to track the good that comes to you between now and Session 8.

Now that you've completed Session 7, begin tithing 7%

Chapter Eight

Before Session 8:

• Read Chapter 8

During Session 8:

• Discuss your experience doing
the activities from Session 7

• Discuss the questions at the end of this chapter

After Session 8:

• Begin tithing 8%

• Do one or more of the activities listed
at the end of this chapter

The Etiquette of Tithing

There is no such thing as charity as popularly understood. Everything belongs to God and all His children are equally entitled to it.

—CHARLES FILLMORE

Tithing raises many questions and pushes many buttons for people. An ongoing debate rages over whether tithing is necessary or whether giving to the needy is a more appropriate way to give in today's times. This creates the illusion that giving or receiving a tithe is an act of charity.

I don't know about you, but many people have a visceral negative reaction to being a "charity case." In fact, the thought of being a charity case keeps many of us from openly receiving our good. Just as there is an art to tithing, there is also an etiquette to tithing to help you work past these obstacles to giving and receiving. Changing this core belief in lack helps you fully embrace and joyfully experience your good.

For starters, some people believe the New Testament of the Bible does away with tithing or that the tithe has been replaced by "a glad offering" or by free will offerings. It is not my intent to dissuade anyone from these beliefs. I merely wish to point out that the difference may be one of semantics. If you find you have a visceral reaction to the word "tithe," stop and examine where this reaction is coming from. You may discover you carry around outdated beliefs about tithing, beliefs that are tied to control issues, which I addressed in the previous chapter.

If you currently have everything you desire, you have great joy in all areas of your life, and give in ways that resonate strongly with you, keep doing what you're doing. Whatever name you call the gifts you give freely, cheerfully, joyfully and willingly, keep giving them with grateful thanksgiving. Tithing by any other name? Still *tithing*!

As you begin practicing the art of tithing—no matter what name you call it—you'll soon discover that what goes around comes around. *As you give, so shall you receive.*

Learning to be a better receiver is vital to learning how to be a better giver. As I pointed out earlier in this book, giving and receiving are exactly the same thing. A mental shift in how you view tithes makes you open and receptive to receiving the good that comes to you. Many people (and I was one of them when I first began tithing!) view tithes as charity or some sort of handout, which our egos view negatively.

Every time you receive, and every time you give, you make it possible for limitless good to flow to both you and the other party. Acknowledge all gifts with gratitude and thanksgiving. When people give to you, it is because they place great value on you!

The meaning of words and phrases evolve over time. I intentionally chose this chapter's opening quote to help you reframe the popular meaning of charity. *There is no such thing as charity, as popularly understood. Everything belongs to God and all His children are equally entitled to it.*

No one is asking for a handout, and you're not giving a handout when you give a tithe. Likewise, you're not receiving a handout. You are simply receiving part of the good God has prepared for you.

Charity, being benevolent, means "doing good or causing good to be done." Our history is filled with "benefactors" who created trust funds or otherwise supported artists, musicians, composers, writers, teachers, ministers, rabbis, and other spiritual leaders so they might be free to reach the masses, according to their talents and missions. These acts of charity brought attention to and provided support for the creative and spiritual work these individuals were doing. Today, much of this benevolent work is done through tax-deductible charities, but much is also given through individuals with no thought to any tax benefit.

Cuban-born artist Rafael Soriano's work in the United States would most likely never have been created if not for a generous benefactor who paid him the equivalent of his wages so he could paint. *To Kill a Mockingbird* would never have been written had Harper Lee not had a benefactor who paid all her bills for a year so she could write full time.

An old Buddhist story tells about a merchant who gave a monk a bag of gold for the improvement of the local monastery. The monk acknowledged the gift, and nothing more. The merchant, expecting gratitude, was bothered. After hinting to the unresponsive monk for a short while, he finally burst out and said, "I just gave you an entire bag of gold! I would think someone who just received such a gift would be thankful!" To which the monk replied with a big grin, "I just accepted a bag of gold. The giver should be thankful."

It's easy to find ourselves expecting an outpouring of verbal gratitude and thanksgiving from those who receive our gifts and tithes. Be on guard when these expectations arise. Remember that tithing is about giving thanks for what we have already been given. It's not about giving in order to get, whether what we're expecting to get is someone's respect, preferential treatment, or merely a "thank you."

Practice tithing with *everything* you give. I've counseled many people who stopped giving gifts to certain people, simply because they never received a thank you note. Proper etiquette indicates a thank you note or call regarding a gift is *appropriate*, but *not* receiving a thank you is no reason to withhold anything. When you withhold your gift because you didn't receive, you're giving to *get*, not to *give* thanks. This simple act takes you out of the flow of your good. I find it useful to assume everyone has already said *thank you*, even if I didn't hear them say it.

Recognize the Constant Flow

As you see, it's important not to block your prosperity by withholding your tithes and gifts. It's equally important not to let others diminish your good by allowing them to refuse your tithe.

I'm often moved by incredible music. The first time I tithed directly to the soloist and the pianist at my home church, they both attempted to turn down the tithe. I simply said, "Please don't stand in the way of my good. You fed my soul and I feel compelled to give you this gift. Please accept it graciously in the spirit in which it is being given." After these simple words of thanks from me, they gladly accepted my tithes.

Some people often turn down their good because they are afraid of appearing needy. Others turn down their good because we've had it drummed into our heads not to accept charity, or money, for doing good deeds. Doing the good deed is supposed to be reward enough. And it is. Accepting a tithe is another good deed.

Accepting a gift is as much a blessing to the giver as the gift is to the receiver. Giving or receiving isn't about balancing the books; it's about maintaining the flow of abundance in your life through a conscious act of giving thanks.

Tap into the circular flow of Universal Energy. Energy must flow in, around and through you or it becomes stagnant. This applies to monetary energy as much as any other energy. Give freely and receive freely or you will put a bottleneck in the universal flow of energy. You stop up the abundance of all you encounter when you react to a gift from a place of fear or shame, whether you're giving or receiving.

When you give, stay open and receptive to gifts offered to you. All blessings shared by others from their income, time, unique abilities, treasures, words, thoughts and deeds are acts of good.

Try this exercise if you are uncomfortable receiving a gift or a tithe. If you're worried someone's gift is too large, too expensive, too much of their time, or comes with strings attached, ask: "Are you sure?" If they say "Yes," say "Thank You" and graciously accept their gift so all may be blessed. The fears we have are *our* fears. This simple question "are you sure?" gives us room to own our fear so we can be more open to receive.

I was once part of an unusual tithing situation that illustrates this concept.

I spent some time with my wonderful spiritual mentor, Nellie Lauth, and tithed to her. Later that evening, I received a tithe from Nellie. I was so grateful for the unexpected tithe, and for how deeply I was moved during that evening's meditation which Nellie led, that I immediately tithed back to Nellie 10% of what I had just received from her.

Sometimes, you and the people in your life will spiritually feed each other. Honor that with your gifts. Don't withhold your gifts because you think it's weird to give back to someone who just tithed to you. At the same time, do not feel obligated to give back to someone who has given to you, unless they have fed your spirit, and you wish to thank them in kind.

It's time to begin to acknowledge that you are always tithing, all day, whether you know it or not. You tithe of your abilities, even in your everyday work world. You tithe of your thoughts, every time you rejoice in someone else's good. You tithe of your words, every time you offer someone encouragement. You tithe of your treasure, every time you joyfully spend money on something.

Give freely, with gratitude and thanksgiving, and stay open and receptive to the good that appears. This good may come in the form of a steady paycheck, a desired weight loss, increased health, a new client, an unexpected opportunity, wonderful gifts or the release of a relationship. Be open and receptive to letting Spirit decide how your good will come to you. Release the fear and open your heart to give and receive.

As you become more in tune with the flow of Universal Abundance, your good will begin to appear in your life in a multitude of ways. Don't turn down this good as charity. People will begin to do things for you, or give you things, and you need to learn how to graciously receive them. Time to break the cycle of sabotaging your good!

After a middle-aged couple had been tithing for several months, they called to say their finances were in worse shape than before. I had them walk me through events from the past few months.

The husband told of how his sister had taken their children out to lunch and had later wanted to take the entire family out to dinner. He told her she couldn't because she had already bought lunch. So he bought dinner for everyone, which cost them a great deal.

Then the wife told of how her in-laws had offered to sit down and review the couple's finances. The in-laws wanted to give them some money to bridge the dry spell they were experiencing as the husband started his new medical practice. They hadn't taken up the in-laws' offer, because they assumed the in-laws couldn't really afford to give the money.

Incredible prosperity opportunities and gifts were unfolding right before their eyes, yet they refused to recognize and accept them. I pointed this out and suggested they acknowledge what they had been doing, coming clean with their relatives. When they mentioned their realization, the helpful relatives were quick to point out many other ways the couple had been turning down their good! Once they stopped turning down their good, their flow improved immensely.

Above all else, have faith. Have faith in the goodness of the work you are doing, in the goodness of the community around you that supports you and your work, and have faith in your own innate goodness.

Give back to God a portion of your good and demonstrate with your actions that you are committed to bringing forth even greater good into your awareness. Then, make known what you desire in your life. Set your intentions and ask for what you desire. Pay attention to where what you *desire* is based on a fear or lack, and where it is based on achieving a goal with passion and purpose.

What is the great goal or "definiteness of purpose" as Napoleon Hill called it, that you wish to achieve in your life? Declare it, and give thanks in advance that what you desire is yours.

The Art of Receiving

"Argue for your limitations and, sure enough, they're yours."
—RICHARD BACH

Are you ready to begin asking the Infinite Intelligence for what you want—trusting that you already have it— or do you want to continue to believe you only have what you can physically see?

A woman had no money in the bank, no cash on hand and no food for lunch one day. She had credit cards, but didn't want to use them; she had committed to not taking on any new debt. Instead, she decided to trust that, in the Universal Flow of life, her lunch had already been provided. At lunchtime, she was still waiting expectantly wondering how her lunch would manifest. She did not wonder *if* it would manifest. She simply wondered *how*.

Would someone offer to take her to lunch or give her their leftovers or what? A half hour into her lunch break she decided, for fun, to go through her wallet just to see what was there. No money, as she thought, just credit cards. But then, she found a gift certificate for a FREE meal at a local chicken place. She was so delighted with her little miracle she laughed aloud and wrote to tell me about it.

Decades ago, an abundance of "coincidences" surrounded a workshop tour I did with a colleague. Anytime we needed, wanted or desired anything, we declared it aloud, and it appeared. We received hotel rooms at specific prices, a glass of Merlot and live music after a long day (which manifested at a *diner* of all places), incredible food, an abundance of cash instead of checks (so we wouldn't have to find a bank in the pre-ATM era), and the right and perfect people attending our seminars.

We became so used to getting everything we desired we would just say, "wouldn't it be nice if..." and then gave it no more thought for the rest of the day. We positively *knew* we were going to get what we desired. We had no fear of not having what we wanted. Just a complete knowing that the Universe had already provided.

One day, while flying to Arizona to speak, we declared, "wouldn't it be nice if.... we could find a place to get a massage?" Imagine our delight when the woman picking us up idly chatted about being in massage school, accumulating "experience credits" for massages. Then she said, "I'd love to give you free massages while you're in town, if you're interested." We gladly accepted, of course!

Ask and expect to receive. What are you going to ask for? What do you truly desire in your life? And how can you build enough trust to know it is already yours?

Don't limit yourself. A woman once gifted me with an all-expense-paid two-week trip to Hawaii as a tithe for my services. Before we got off the phone, she asked, "Is there anything else you need today?" Without thinking, I immediately reverted to limited thinking and said, "Oh, no, you've done quite enough already." Oddly enough, the trip never materialized.

She willingly, cheerfully and joyfully extended a gift, which I batted down. I assumed she asked out of politeness, when in fact she was offering me a part of my limitless abundance. It reminded me of my youthful decision to harvest the raspberries once a week. Because I turned down my good, the abundant good never materialized.

After that, I learned never to make assumptions, and to always receive tithes cheerfully.

A regular tither demonstrated the prospering power of affirmative prayers when she sat down at her desk and began writing out the affirmation "*Everything and everybody prospers me now."* She had written it four times when a co-worker came by and randomly handed her a $25 PetSmart gift card. She used it to get her dog's nails clipped and buy him some toys and treats. I see this happen all the time. Receiving through giving is a paradox of tithing. When you give, you naturally open yourself up to receive.

The minister of a severely indebted church suggested that his church members tithe. His suggestion was soundly voted down. He then asked them to try tithing for one month. At month's end, those who heartily entered into the agreement and were giving thanks with their tithes were prospering abundantly. Those who grudgingly tithed admitted they had held their own. The members agreed to tithe another six months, after which point the church was debt-free and had begun rebuilding savings.

A single mother with four children tithed from her first minimum wage paycheck. As she continued tithing, her salary increased. One year later, her salary was nearly eight times her original salary.

A contractor tithed faithfully and his business was always booming. Another contractor on his block did equally good work but didn't believe in tithing. He rarely had enough work to stay busy and often hired himself out to his neighbor. The only apparent difference between the two men was that one gave thanks with everything he gave and the other did not.

One man began tithing ten dollars a month and continued tithing as his income grew. When his tithe grew to one hundred dollars a month, this seemed too much to tithe and he stopped tithing altogether. Disaster followed in all areas of his life until he again began to tithe.

Set Your Intentions

Don't pray for more—pray for a greater awareness
of how the omnipresent abundance of the Universe
is manifest in your life, here and now.
—PAULA LANGGUTH RYAN (OH, WAIT, THAT'S ME!)

Achieving the realization that everything is working out perfectly—even when it doesn't match our idea of what *perfect* is supposed to be—is one of the highest levels of consciousness we can achieve. As you give, so shall you receive. Give not out of guilt or fear, but give in whatever way you're spiritually led to give.

When you receive, focus on receiving from a place of love, gratitude and thankfulness and not from guilt or fear. In gratitude, you will quickly discover limitless bounty exists for you. Large and small demonstrations will abound as you give thanks with your tithes and take your place in the ever flowing abundance by gratefully receiving all that is offered to you. Allow yourself to experience your limitlessness. It's the greatest gift you can give yourself.

Here's a sampling of the non-monetary abundance offered to people who shared their stories with me during just one two-week period:

- free tickets to "The Big E, " New England's fair
- a large bagful of thermal underwear
- free raspberries, potatoes, beets, tomatoes, squash and pickles
- free auto parts (this particularly excited me because it was the first time this new tither recognized the results of her tithing!)
- a free salad
- free dresses
- a $417 discount on new brakes
- free massages
- potted plants
- thousands of dollars of technical computer support
- free honey
- free ironing
- a free modem card
- free books
- free music
- spiritual breakthroughs
- an outpouring of creative ideas

- free dog food, dog care and boarding
- healing relationships with loved ones
- discounts on rental equipment
- new clients
- effortless interactions with people who seemed to go out of their way to prosper them
- unexpected income
- free Mets tickets (a gift everyone but Yankee fans would appreciate!)
- the resolution of an ongoing financial challenge
- peace of mind about current stock market investments
- the perfect dinner companion
- . . . and so much more!

By giving, you open yourself up to receive. By being willing to receive, you create incredible circulation of good in all areas of your life.

Once you're ready and willing to experience this outpouring of greater good in your life, write down what you desire in the form of an intention. See yourself having what you desire, and know your desire is manifest in your life in ways that are always for your highest good. I recommend ending your intention with the phrase: "*This or something better, and so it is, for the highest good of all. Thank you, God!*"

Below, I've listed some sample intentions for different areas of your life, to help you set your intentions. Many are actual intentions my students have held in prayer, to manifest what they desired in their lives.

Follow Your Life Purpose/ Releasing Fear

I see myself open and receptive to the knowledge that God, and only God, is the source of my good!

I see my highest good revealed to me!

I see myself joyfully sharing my blessings with all I encounter!

I see everyone effortlessly supporting me!

I see myself stepping out in faith, releasing all fear and doubt, and embracing the love I deserve and desire, from myself and from others!

I see myself on track in every area of my life, as I become open and receptive to the knowledge that I deserve all the abundance that flows to me!

I see myself at peace with the unfolding of events!

All that I desire is now mine as I make myself open and receptive, giving and receiving love in all areas of my life!

I see myself examining, understanding, embracing and effortlessly living my truth!

I see myself secure and at peace!

I see myself blessed with the knowledge needed to manifest my heart's desires!

I see myself open and receptive to my heart's desires!

I see myself fully embracing my Divine Intelligence, secure in the knowledge my desires are mine already, waiting to be claimed by me!

I see myself knowing, with absolute certainty, that I am in the right and perfect place in my life and on the right and perfect path!

I see myself open and receptive to embracing myself and my life fully, right now!

I see everything in my life unfolding in divine timing!

I see myself released from my fears and doubts!

Create Intentional Relationships

I see myself ever blessed, loved and loving in all my interactions with others!

I see the right and perfect romantic relationship becoming visible to me as I make myself open and receptive to giving and receiving love in all areas of my life!

I see myself having the wedding of my dreams at the right and perfect price!

I see myself open and receptive to healing my relationship now!

I see myself released from all fears, able and willing to communicate lovingly and openly to resolve existing relationship issues and create a lasting, loving partnership now!

I see myself open and receptive to being of right service to all those whose lives cross my path!

I see myself releasing and blessing all those I misperceive to have caused me harm. As I forgive, I give; and as I give, I receive blessings!

I see myself inspired, creative, and able to implement my ideas as I interact with others!

I see the right and perfect relationship appearing as I step out in faith and become the perfect partner I wish to have!

I freely and fully forgive everyone in all my past relationships, including myself. I am open and receptive to experiencing the right and perfect relationship now!

Live an Effortless, Debt Free and Prosperous Life

I see myself freely giving and receiving from the bounty the Universe has provided me with today and every day!

I see myself incurring no debt for what I desire. I see everything falling into place effortlessly, in divine timing, in divine order!

I see myself open and receptive to receiving $10,000 worth of abundance or more, now, as I become open and receptive to the knowledge that I deserve all the abundance available to me!

I see my savings and investments growing effortlessly, every day, building the right and perfect nest egg for me!

I see myself firmly planted in the flow of peace and prosperity!

I see all my finances in perfect order now!

I see my financial situation improving easily and effortlessly, every day!

I see myself ever prospered in all I do!

I see myself released from my fears and my debts!

I see myself current with all my bills and rapidly paying off all my debts!

I see myself owing no one anything but love!

I see myself completely free from all my debts!

I see myself released from all obligations to others as I release all others from their obligations to me, seeing them ever prospered!

Enjoy Peaceful Transitions

I see this change as a prosperous and abundant change, in all ways!

I see myself in the right and perfect new situation!

I see myself embracing the good that is in my life today, making room for the greater good to become visible!

I see myself as a free spirit, welcoming change!

I see myself living peacefully with the chaos around me, trusting in the process!

I see myself selling my home effortlessly, for the right and perfect price!

I see the right and perfect outcome to this situation unfolding in my life now!

Build a Joyful Career/Business

I see the right and perfect opportunity appearing in my life now and I see myself effortlessly taking action on that opportunity, secure in the knowledge that everything is unfolding in divine order, in divine timing and for the highest good of all!

I see myself effortlessly and joyfully enjoying my new success and my increased income in a positive way, using my greater good to bless others as I have been blessed!

I see myself stepping out in faith to do the work I love, secure in the knowledge that all my needs are always met, abundantly!

I see myself enjoying a fulfilling and prosperous job!

I see myself excelling in my new work!

I see my new business growing effortlessly and prosperously!

I see happy customers effortlessly drawn to my positive energy and my attitude of service!

I see an endless stream of referrals in my business now!

I see my business growing effortlessly every day, in every way, as I open myself up to the divine flow of good that is fully present in my life!

I see myself open, receptive and ready to step out in faith, releasing my attachment to my job as the source of my good!

I see people effortlessly drawn to me, valuing me and my work and prospering me now!

Experience Overflowing Health and Vitality

I see myself whole, healed and healthy, in all areas of my life!

I see every area of my life in complete balance now, with an abundance of time to work out, meditate and relax!

I see myself filled with divine light, energy, peace, love and joy!

I see the right and perfect healing in my life now!

I see my body as flexible and strong, and I delight in my vibrant health!

I see myself releasing weight rapidly, permanently and in a healthy manner!

This or something better now manifests for the highest good of all. And so it is. Thank you, God!

What's Your Intention?

People often write to share their intentions. I hold intentions in prayer for 30 days, then write to see what has manifested in their lives.

Are you ready to set your intention for what you desire? Write out your intention and send me a copy. I'll gladly hold your intention in prayer for you for 30 days. The power of prayer is always magnified whenever two or more people are gathered in prayer.

Intentions may be sent to:

Paula Langguth Ryan

PO Box 7530, Denver, CO 80207

Session 8 Questions for Discussion

1. In the past, where have you been attached to your good coming from? What attachments are you willing to give up?

2. What steps did you take toward things you previously thought you "couldn't afford" to do?

3. How did it feel to begin easily and effortlessly setting aside 1% of your income to put toward a desire you've always had?

4. What abundance have you received as a result of giving freely from your possessions?

5. What major desires have you been trying to realize in your life? What steps are you willing to take today—financially and in every other way—to bring you closer to your desire, no matter how small those steps?

6. Where have you taken advantage of others or been untrustworthy in your life?

7. Where are you willing to give more in your life, in order to get more?

8. What disharmony (unspoken anger, fear, resentment or sadness) are you willing to resolve in your personal life or professional life, in order to create greater abundance?

9. Do this **In Class Exercise** (continue on your own at home each day): Get quiet and into a meditative space. Bring to mind each person in your life, as they come into your consciousness and affirm:

> *Let me see this person and this situation rightly. Let me see this person and this situation as Divine Love in Action. Let me see myself as Divine Love in Action. I release and bless this person and this situation from all that I misperceived to have occurred. I bless and support everyone involved in all their power and magnificence. Divine Love, IN me, AS me, IS me—in this and every situation. And so it is!*

As you affirm, make a conscious choice to let go of any perceived hurt, let go of the need to be right, and allow yourself to heal and be happy instead. Consciously see each person or situation blessed for their highest good, even in situations your ego perceives as a grievance.

Session 8 Activities (do one or more after Session 8)

1. Continue to do the **In Class Exercise** from this chapter.

2. Make a list of the attachments you have to *how* your good comes to you. Circle any you are willing to release.

3. Make a list of all the people and places from which you've ever received abundance, in any form.

4. Between now and Session 9, when you find yourself having expectations about whether or not something will turn out the way you desire, stop yourself and affirm: *I can't wait to discover how I will see this good in my life!*

5. Every night write down—or mentally give thanks for—at least 25 people, places, experiences, etc. that occurred in your life today. Start each one with "I am grateful for. . . ."

6. Make a list of everyone you feel has ever held you back professionally, personally or financially. Make a list of why you are grateful for that person or situation—what you learned, what gifts you gained from that encounter. Thank them for their contributions, which have brought you to this right and perfect moment in your life. *(Bonus: write and send them a gratitude letter!)*

7. Set an intention to help yourself embrace your divine inheritance, in 25 words or less. For example: *"Divine Love, IN me, AS me, IS me. This Divine*

Love that I AM blesses and multiplies all that I am, do, experience and give." Repeat this intention throughout the day, whenever your mind wanders to negative thoughts of lack or limitation.

8. Select three desires you want to perceive in your life. Notice and write down exactly what you desire and any action you take around these desires, no matter how small the movement appears.

9. Continue your gift recording journal, assigning a monetary value to everything you receive.

10. Continue giving something away to someone every day.

11. Continue holding each person's intention in prayer.

12. Continue watching your language.

13. Use a fresh *Prosperity Tracker* to track the good that comes to you.

Now that you've completed Session 8, begin tithing 8%

Chapter Nine

Before Session 9:
- Read Chapter 9

During Session 9:
- Discuss your experience doing the activities from Session 8
- Discuss the questions at the end of this chapter

After Session 9:
- Begin tithing 9%
- Do one or more of the activities listed at the end of this chapter

Expanding Your View of Prosperity

Everything and everybody prospers me now.

—CATHERINE PONDER

Tithing in all areas of your life means becoming a "prepper." Preparing for incredible wisdom, success, health, joy, love, financial wealth and an outpouring of abundance in all areas of your life. Are you ready? Can you conceive of having more good in your life, or are you trapped in the cycle of *wishing* you had more good in your life?

How would you react if you suddenly found your income doubling? What would you do with your new-found income? How would you change? How would you react if you suddenly had everything you ever wanted, right now, and with every need or desire fulfilled instantly? How strong are your values? Would you continue to hold onto your scarcity models of what your life *will* look like? Would you always be waiting for the other shoe to drop? Or would you expand your feelings about abundance beyond anything you could possibly imagine for yourself?

These are very serious questions. I encourage you to stop a moment, grab a pad of paper and write down your answers to the above questions.

Many people have problems being receptive to gifts, no matter how sincere, because they fear there are strings attached. You may think that such gifts mean you will "owe them one." You may have even grown up in an environment where you believed gifts were given with strings attached. Regardless of the perceived intentions of the giver, *you* can receive with a full heart.

A man who came to this new way of thinking started unblocking things he didn't even know were blocked. With his newfound understanding of receiving, he accepted an offer from a co-worker who took him out for lunch one day, out of the blue. As a result, he gained a lot of insight about how his co-worker's department worked that he wouldn't have gotten otherwise.

Use the information I've given you about receiving. Use it on your own intellectual and emotional blocks to open up new channels of good. Turn those blocks into stepping stones on your new pathway of prosperity. Think about stones a minute.

Each stone, by itself, is fairly useless; ugly, gray—an obstacle. Harness the stones' energy by putting them all together, however, and you can build many things of beauty: a stone fence, bench, the foundation for a waterfall, towering spires of a grand cathedral, or a pathway.

The beauty of a stone is in how you perceive it. It's time to start seeing the intellectual and emotional blocks you're dealing with as individual stepping stones on your road to progress instead of as roadblocks. We go through so much of our lives in a state of conscious unconsciousness.

These stepping stones—these perceived road-blocks—jostle us into examining our present circum-stances and beliefs. Revealing to us what still holds true for us and what no longer serves us.

A woman who tithes regularly began feeling a pros-perity pinch—and it was pinching enough that it hurt a bit. I reminded her of the prosperity basics. I challenged her to become like King Solomon, the richest and wis-est man in the Bible, who only ever asked God for divine ideas!

She took her challenge into prayer and meditation. That evening she began having very inspired ideas about freeing up the Divine Flow in her life. She acted as guided—without attachment or expectation—and experienced wonderful tangible results within weeks. These included:

- a house clearing which dramatically changed the energy in her home
- an unexpected $500 check from a relative
- the gift of over $100 worth of herbal tinctures for detoxification and draining (she had wanted to purchase them but thought she couldn't afford the expense)
- the reclaiming of a "junk" room in her house which has become a sanctuary for her
- the most amazing chocolate chip cookies
- improved communications with almost everyone in her life, and
- clarity about issues that blocked effective communications in her relationships

She also benefited from the movement of hundreds of dollars' worth of products she had been "holding onto." A renewed burst of creativity inspired her to create new classes and co-create teaching opportunities which morphed into the creation of new products. She also experienced an incredible sense of limitless love and boundless possibilities in her life.

Her intellectual and emotional roadblocks all became stepping stones. They raised her awareness and caused her to recommit to remembering that she is always in the flow, despite what appearances might indicate. Through this experience she came to truly believe that her abundance encompasses so much more than her bank account balance.

Have you ever "lost" your keys in a room that you hadn't left? The keys were always there, even though they weren't visible to you, right? That's the perfect metaphor for the abundance in your life. All the abundance in the universe is already present in your life, even when it's not visible to you. Your task is to get still and listen for your guidance. You get an idea of an action to take. You're guided to sit down, pick up your newspaper and voila, there are your car keys!

Ideas may be the most profitable gift you will ever receive, once you begin giving thanks with your tithes. You will soon discover that, like King Solomon, your best action is to ask for guidance instead of a specific outcome. Instead of giving you fish, God teaches you *how* to fish. Instead of giving you an immediate cash infusion (although this does happen), you may find your prosperity in the form of new and wonderful ideas. Take one step at a time to put those ideas into action.

And do I need to say it? Take action with no attachments or expectations.

A woman began tithing again after reading my monthly newsletter. She discovered firsthand how tithing of time and money really does work. Doors immediately began opening for her, putting her in touch with people who could help her with her new business venture. Bringing her clarity and healing in her relationship with her mother, who in turn bestowed a financial blessing toward her new business. Her mother even encouraged *her* friends to financially support this new business.

As she discovered, when you speak your desires into the Universe, they come to pass. Think of it this way: You pull up in the drive-thru of a fast food restaurant. You speak your desires when you place your order, talking to the invisible source within. You move forward, and then, *voila*, your order is handed to you.

Tithing provides a constant reminder of our connection to the Infinite Intelligence from which all good comes. When you tithe with gratitude and appreciation—when you give thanks—you focus your attention on that Source, on that Infinite Intelligence, and become open and receptive to receiving your rich, abundant supply.

Honor Yourself Enough
to Stay the Course

God is with those who persevere.

—THE KORAN

Sometimes, honoring our commitments to ourselves and to the Source that supplies all good in our lives is simply a matter of having the courage of our convictions. We must honor ourselves enough to stay focused on our goal, to persevere no matter what.

A woman had very negative feelings associated with tithes due to her religious upbringing but she decided to start tithing to see how it worked. She immediately tithed to someone who provided her with spiritual support and peace.

After a few weeks she realized her financial situation was improving. She could not identify *how* her financial situation could be improving; she hadn't received any increase in income. She just felt better about her financial situation and herself.

After a few months she stopped tithing. Sure enough, her financial situation changed and within a year she had amassed $15,000 in debt. She again decided to start tithing and immediately wrote a check for 10% of what she had in the bank and once again began tithing 10%

of her paycheck. She felt wonderful and, after just a few days, she sensed that things were looking up.

Even though her income had not increased, she was again able to pay her bills and her money seemed to be lasting longer than in the past.

We all learn the benefits of tithing at our own pace. We all come to our own expanded awareness of good, even if we're surrounded by people who tithe. After many years of listening to me joyfully talk about the art of tithing, my dear friend Janet vibrantly demonstrated that giving with faith and joy is an important step to receiving greater good.

Janet wanted to tithe to her local homeless shelter, but she felt her tithe would leave her "almost" broke for a week. Eventually, she stepped out in faith, saying, "God, you'll make sure I'm taken care of if I tithe this amount." She wrote her tithe check and that afternoon received a new client. Every day since she wrote the check, something new and wonderful has happened to her and her business.

She vowed to never again put off her tithing and vowed to tithe faithfully every month with an open heart and a prayer of thanks.

A massage therapist who daily practices the art of tithing rolls any missed tithes into her next day's tithe. She has fun mailing out checks, no matter the amount, and every time she puts an envelope in the mail, she gets another call for massage therapy work.

A woman tithed and made her desire known for increased prosperity in her flower shop. She loves doing floral arrangements for weddings, and was amazed at how many weddings she booked in the month after her first tithe. She received her increased prosperity by doing what she loved.

How will you know when it's time to step out in faith? When you begin to remember that everything is in Divine Order. When you're willing to feel the fear and do it anyway. When you're ready to commit to having a good time in your life—no matter what expected or unexpected results occur.

Commit to having a good time with your tithes, in every area of your life. Of course, this means letting go of your expectations of the outcome. Yes, you may desire a certain outcome. But as *A Course In Miracles* so eloquently states: *You do not know your own best interests.* Most of what we think is best for us is wrapped up in fear or cultural conditioning.

I encourage you to simply affirm that the outcome—*or something better*—has already occurred, and then step out in faith. Every mile is walked one step at a time. A swing soars higher, one push at a time. All journeys begin this way.

How do we learn to put one foot in front of the other? How do we learn to push a swing at just the right time? Trial and error. Not every attempt is perfect. Seek progress, not perfection. Ask anyone who's jammed a finger pushing a swing too soon, or felt their fingertips barely brush the back of the person on the swing because they've pushed too late. Ask any toddler who's taking those first tentative steps. It's all trial and error.

But what keeps us trying? What keeps us moving forward and using each next opportunity to take those steps or to push the swing again? Hope. Hope and a commitment to honor ourselves by having a good time playing on the playground. Life is your own personal playground. Make a commitment, starting today, to have a good time with the rest of your life.

Bless everything in your life, especially when you spend money. Discover the great joy in giving thanks for what your bills represent—and you will soon stop dreading the arrival of your mail or unexpected expenses.

When you sit down and pay your electric bill, spend a moment of quality time thinking about what your money represents. It represents the electricity that keeps the fridge running, so you don't have to worry about your food spoiling and you can have ice cream with your children. It represents the air conditioning or heat that keeps your home comfortable. It represents the power to your computer that allows you to reach out across the world and meet new people and learn new things.

What does your car repair bill really represent? It represents freedom to come and go to as you please, to visit friends, be alone at the beach, get to the doctors, transport your kids in safety, and so on.

How much are those blessings really worth? The money per gallon you pay for gas doesn't just pay for the fuel that gets you around. It also pays the taxes for smooth roads that provide you with a gentle drive, and road signs that get you where you're going (or help you get un-lost if you're like me!), and so on.

What are these pleasures really worth? If your electric bill is $150 this month, did you get $150 worth of enjoyment, peace of mind, serenity and fun out of your electricity? I usually find the value I place on my enjoyment is ten times what I'm actually paying. The next time you pay for something, *joyfully* complete the financial exchange, and thank the Universe for all the gifts that bill represents. Like me, you may soon discover that paying your bills becomes just another form of tithing.

Bless everyone you come into contact with. Bless them and see them receiving their heart's desires.

A woman hated being at work because of two co-workers who constantly complained about everything. She began seeing her co-workers happily working in their right and perfect jobs—somewhere else. Within three months, both complaining co-workers had gotten new jobs elsewhere and her workplace once again became a joyful place to be.

Incorporate simple affirmations into your day, like:

I see gold dust in the air! (a good affirmation when springtime pollen flies everywhere!)

Every day, in every way, I see my abundance growing and growing and growing, thank you God!

God is the Source of my supply.

I let go and trust the Universe to provide.

If you find your prosperity consciousness drifting off center, remind yourself of this:

1) Everything happening in your life is happening for a reason,

2) The reason something is happening is *always* for your highest good—even if you can't *see* the good in the moment.

Use a phrase like, "Thank you, God!" whenever something happens in your life, no matter what it is. Other effective phrases include, "It's all Good," or "This is for my highest good." Or even my favorite, "Awesome!"

Get a flat tire? *Awesome!* Get cut off in traffic? *Thank you, God.* Someone lets you into traffic? *Awesome!* Forget to return your library book? *This is for my highest good.*

Library fine gets forgiven? *Thank you, God.* Computer crashes? *It's all Good.* Someone gives you a check for $300? *It's all Good.* Someone gives you a bill for $300? *It's all Good.* Have a fight with a family member? *It's for my highest good.* Get praised at work? *It's for my highest good.* Get your car broken into? *It's for my highest good.* You get the idea?

No matter what happens, give thanks for the event and *know* this event is bringing you closer to where you're supposed to be. Even something we declare as being "tragic" carries hidden blessings. When you are completely overwhelmed, use the phrase, "No matter what anyone else meant this for, God meant it for good." Know that everything that happens in your life and everyone who comes into your life is here to help you heal, grow, and become the best you can be.

Turn tithing into an intentional game of thanksgiving. Actively seek out people who feed your spirit and tithe to them. When you smile or chuckle to yourself over something you see, read or hear immediately ask yourself: who can I thank for this gift? Give the first tenth of your income, give of your time, your abilities, possessions, words, thoughts and actions.

Above all else, though, give freely, willingly and joyfully. Remember the man who paid his bills instead of paying his $400 tithe? The Universe quickly responded to the gratitude in his first tithe by opening up new and exciting channels of good for him. Divine Flow was established, and he stepped into it effortlessly and was amply rewarded. Then he turned around and forgot to give thanks for the new prosperity that had manifest. He wasn't a good steward of the abundance handed him, and suddenly the flow stopped. When it did, he became engulfed by fear.

When you find yourself faced with fear over a decision of whether to tithe or pay a bill that's coming due, I encourage you to take the leap of faith, tithe and stay focused on reality: God is the Source of All Your Good. You'll quickly discover that your faith is more than amply rewarded.

A man was inspired to step out in faith and began sharing what God had given him. He was scared. He was deeply in debt and didn't have enough to pay his necessary expenses, but he had faith. He could see many doors opening, and had faith that his good would appear, even though his prosperity had not yet manifested in a form visible to him.

I shared with him this affirmation: *I am fearless in letting money go out, knowing God is my immediate and endless supply.*

Three months later he shared what was occurring in his life. He had made more money in the previous three months than ever before, and felt more joyful and open to new experiences. He had become more willing to go for what he wants and more willing to spend money on things that help him grow. When a month starts out slowly, he reminds himself that God is the source of all abundance and has already given him what he has asked for, even if he doesn't know how it will appear.

This man began affirming that he was making at least $4,000 a month and by the end of the month he had come to within a couple hundred dollars of that goal. When he counted his gross abundance (not just the dollars he received), he was way above his goal.

Today, he is constantly receiving little gifts and signs of God's Love. Life feels more in tune with the Universe. He has paid off all his peripheral debts and now only has one debt to pay back. I am certain that, within a year, he will be completely debt free.

When you step out in faith and give in the face of apparent lack, you show the Universe you can be a good and faithful steward of Infinite Abundance. Once you give thanks with your tithe, be still for a moment. Stay present and receptive to whatever comes. Step out in faith that God is providing you with all you desire, for your highest good. Honor yourself. Set clear intentions of what you want, make those desires known, and step out in faith knowing—with absolute certainty—that what you seek is already given to you and will appear in divine timing in a way that is for your highest good.

Tithing out of a sense of joy, thankfulness and gratitude breathes new life into your giving; you'll find yourself *giving to get* less often. See tithing as a joyful opportunity to express your thanks and good will flow into your life effortlessly. View tithing as an effort or an obligation, and you'll receive with effort and a sense of obligation. Life was never meant to be a struggle. We don't have to live with disappointment.

Give with joy, give with faith and give with love. Tithe in all ways and then watch and see if God doesn't expand you and pour *you* out—a blessing that cannot be contained (see my audio lecture on the *Truth About Giving and Receiving* for more about this concept). All around you channels of good will open, allowing you to accomplish even more than you'd originally desired.

Within thirteen months, a woman went from having over $13,000 in unsecured debt to being completely debt free and achieving her dream of a fabulous California vacation. She didn't think it was possible, yet she was willing to hold onto the idea that it *might* be possible. And it *was*!

Many people have shared success stories of how they're now able to follow their true life purpose. It's wonderful to see the power of tithing at work in a collective way, creating an economy where people get paid to do work that feeds their souls. Give to channels that feed your soul and the Universe responds by providing you with your own overflowing helping of soul food.

A woman occasionally experienced clients who appeared to not respect her time and energy, or forgot to pay their bills on time. When she let go of her attachment to the situation and the client, she often discovered a better client waiting in the wings. She would never have had time, space or energy for the new client if she hadn't let go of the old one.

This woman was experiencing the effects of the Divine Law of Prosperity. When you release something from your life that no longer serves you—whether it's a person, a debt, or the outcome to a situation—release it with gratitude for the role it played in your life. In this way, you honor and value your true inner worth, just as you honor and value your spiritual Source when you release your tithe. Honor the situation. It was there for a reason and may no longer be necessary in your life. By honoring and valuing yourself in this way and eliminating resentments and negative thinking that restrain your time and energy, you create a vacuum for new good.

Walking away from situations that no longer feed your spirit—particularly when they're in the form of money providers—can be daunting. Do not view these money providers as the Source of your security. They are merely one *channel* that provides you with a connection to the Source of your true, infinite security.

A woman began walking away from good-paying opportunities that weren't feeding her soul. As she took this leap of faith, she had to confront her fears about money and security, and where the income would come from to replace the potential income she'd just released. In doing this inner work, she opened up the possibility for new, greater opportunities to arrive—and they began arriving right on schedule.

When you let go of what's not working and make room for something new to appear—without any knowledge of what that might be—you're stepping out in faith. You're stepping out in the belief (consciously or unconsciously) that there *will be* something better.

Many people accidentally stumble upon this prosperity principle. It's all about creating a vacuum for more good to flow into. Common wisdom says nature abhors a vacuum. I believe nature loves a vacuum. Think about it. When you loath something, you move away from it. When you love something, you rush toward it. The Universe's natural response is to put something into motion to fill up the empty space.

People usually get so fed up with being treated as "less than" that they throw up their hands and walk away from a situation, with an attitude of "I don't know if what I truly desire is out there but I know *this* isn't it." They fully surrender and walk away from jobs, clients, relationships—you name it—and then what they truly deserve appears in their lives.

Do not get so focused on trying to change the problem into what you think you *do* deserve that you miss the good when it appears in your life. Do not be so fearful of making a mistake you fail to act when what you truly deserve and desire appears. You may be familiar with the phrase: "If it's too good to be true, it probably is." This is almost certainly the number one reason people miss the good in their lives. Do not use the above phrase to justify not taking action in the face of fear. Do not use it to avoid the hard acts of everyday courage that will propel you toward success.

Giving thanks—true tithing—is the greatest act of everyday courage you can imagine, especially when you're working through the fears of giving and receiving. Tithing is by far the simplest, most direct way to achieve success in all areas of your life. It is simple, but it is not easy. Changing your thoughts is hard work; make no mistake about it.

It is far easier to pick up the remote control and click on the television, or mindlessly browse Facebook, YouTube, Twitter or Instagram, or engage in idle gossip bemoaning the fate of the world or others around you. Instead, sit quietly and consciously hold the thought that only good can come from a situation, that this good is manifest already to fill your desires, and will be revealed in divine timing. What's happening around you at any given time is merely what's happening. How you feel about those events is another matter.

True tithing requires you to hold a consciousness of thankfulness in all that you do, all that you say and all that you think. All. Giving thanks requires you to find the hidden blessing in every event and give voice to that blessing. You are continually reaping the fruits of your words and your actions. As you sow, so shall you reap.

A woman who was moving to the United States tithed fearlessly, even though her only income was from a part-time teaching job. Her desire was for the right and perfect price for a plane ticket from her home in Spain to her new home in the United States. Not only did she manifest a $300 ticket during the prime travel season, she manifested gifts to pay for the deeply discounted ticket.

Measuring Your Success

When you measure your abundance in the actual *cash* that flows in your life, you wind up overlooking a great deal of your abundance. In one 30 day period, I received the following: thousands of dollars worth of fantastic clothing, including a floor-length, fully-beaded, backless, emerald green evening gown; food; meals out; airline tickets; traveling accommodations; flowers; a free vacation; concerts; office assistance; more clothes (and fashion guidance!); a four-day Landmark Forum course; Mary Kay products; a fabulous drum; ice cream; spiritual counseling; a channeling session; gourmet meals; massages and original art.

The list went on and on. This is an example of how the Universe opens up and supports you when you step out in faith, perform your services with loving kindness, let go of your attachment to the outcome, ask for what you desire and always give thanks for what you have received.

Even greater than the gifts you receive and the gifts you give is the growth you will experience as a result of tithing. As you practice giving and receiving without attachments or expectations, you will notice you're making fewer judgments.

During the month I received the above gifts, I had very little cash flow. If I measured success by judging the appearance of my checkbook balance, I wasn't being very successful. The outpouring of abundance in my life was quite evident, however, when I focused on the big picture.

We carry around our preconceived notions of what is success or failure, what is good or bad and what is right or wrong, because someone else taught us to believe these things. The truth is, everything that God created just *is*. There is nothing that is good or bad, but *you* make it so. There are only things and events. You make the judgment of what's good or bad based on your beliefs and assumptions.

Think about it. Think about a time when you heard music that didn't resonate with you. You immediately judged it as bad. You labeled it as off key, or nothing but noise, or untalented. You gave it a label: "bad music." Yet there are others who love that type of music. (Sometimes you may even extend your label to the people who love that music and say "they don't know good music.")

Consciously or unconsciously, we tend to label everything. You label art, you label yard sale items. You label people's behavior and people's beliefs. You label experiences. All these labels were taught to us, consciously or unconsciously. For instance, we aren't born with a fear of dogs. Yet many children become afraid of all dogs at an early age. They believe dogs will hurt them because someone taught them to be afraid of dogs or someone reinforced this fear after the child was hurt one time by one dog.

Our thoughts, words and actions are the most impressive teachers we have. Through our thoughts, words and actions, we teach children to be afraid or hate so many things. We teach children to hate bills, to be afraid of failure, to hate what they don't understand, to hate delays or things that don't turn out the way they expect them to turn out, to be afraid their own talents and abilities won't be "good enough" to impress someone else, or to support themselves financially.

Fortunately, we can also use our thoughts, words and actions to teach children to embrace life. Realign your attitudes with the truth: *Nothing is good or bad, but that we make it so.* This enables you to tap into the limitless abundance that's already readily available to you. True prosperity—true, radiant abundance—starts with the knowledge that your thoughts make you a co-creator of the good in your life.

A woman went home after tithing at my seminar and found $5 in the back pocket of her jeans as she was undressing. The next day, while pumping gas she received nearly $20 too much in change. The gas attendant was very thankful for her immediate correction of the error. By taking right action, she kept herself in the flow of abundance, as was evidenced a few days later when she received a notice from the IRS. They were sending her an unexpected $500 refund. This woman also discovered, with great appreciation, that her 14-year-old daughter already lives prosperity principles and vowed to learn from her child how to embrace and give thanks for the abundance in her life.

Here are a few more of the countless stories others have shared.

A woman tithed *once* and within a week her income multiplied tenfold so that her new tithe was ten times her original tithe. The prospering power of 10, the tithe in action, once again!

A man wanted to manifest increased business for his engraving company. The first night he tithed he received an order from a new client for eight plaques.

A full-time musician, continually faced with financial challenges and anxiety, often found herself living 'hand to mouth.' One day, she decided to put on her 'faith' cap and chose to change her perspective about money. She began tithing and giving thanks for the abundance in her life. The more she chose to use the word 'challenge' instead of 'problem' when she spoke and thought about money, the more money came. And it still does.

A woman stated her intention to fulfill a lifelong dream of visiting Mali, Africa and to get a great bargain on her airfare. After tithing for twelve weeks, what she had held in mind manifested the day she'd set as a deadline. Before she left for her trip she was able to manifest an even better bargain. She is a shining symbol of the prospering power of tithing.

Don't Forget to Breathe!

I can feel the magic floating in the air!
—Faith Hill

Remember, tithing is like breathing. What's more natural than breathing? All the air you will ever need already surrounds you. You inhale, effortlessly, and air comes rushing in, time after time. But if you hold your breath and refuse to let the air in, you could suffocate. The air is there, but you believe you lack air because you choose not to let it in.

What happens when you finally stop trying to hold your breath? You let go of the air you were holding onto and new, fresh air comes rushing in. Big gasping gulps of air, more abundant, more pure, and carried more deeply into your lungs. This is what happens when you finally stop withholding your tithe.

In times of stress, it's easy to forget to breathe. Your breathing becomes rapid and shallow, or you exhale and forget to inhale again. Sometimes you need to consciously remember—or have someone remind you—to breathe. Just breathe. So it is with remembering that the substance of abundance is already present in your life, everywhere. So it is with remembering to tithe.

Sometimes you will forget to breathe in the abundance that surrounds you at all times. Luckily, you can breathe substance deep into your mind with thoughts of abundance just as easily as you breathe air into your lungs. Sooner or later, breathing substance in through your thoughts and breathing substance out through your tithes will become as natural an activity as breathing air in and out of your lungs. You'll then begin to manifest in visible form untold riches. Don't be afraid to breathe in the abundance that is rightfully yours. Breathe it all in, and breathe out your thanks and gratitude every day, and in every way.

Expanding your prosperity consciousness is as simple as expanding your lung capacity. The more abundance you make room for in your life, the more you will experience.

My dear friend (and fellow chocolate-lover) Beth once gifted me with a ticket to a sneak preview of the Oscar-bound movie, *Chocolat*, while I was visiting her in Manhattan. The strength of the main character, Vianne Rocher (played by Juliette Binoche), stuck with me. A wayfaring chocolatier, Vianne is repeatedly judged and found guilty of a myriad of sins in every situation she finds herself. Yet she has the courage of her convictions and the inner fortitude to stay the course and honor herself, even when the obstacles in her path seem insurmountable.

As one reviewer put it, Vianne "set off a confrontation between those who would keep life the same and those who would revel in their newly discovered taste for freedom."

As you change and grow and begin to practice the art of tithing in all you do, people around you may not always appear supportive. We are all human, and as humans, we dislike change, as a rule. Our natural inclination is to take action to prevent change from taking place. Do not be dismayed or disheartened when this happens. Stay the course. Be strong; be courageous in your convictions.

To achieve your goals, you must stay the course and be true to your heart's desire and continue to tithe, no matter how many obstacles, no matter how many heartbreaks and heartaches and fears and setbacks get in your way. They are showing up to help you heal your limited beliefs and embrace the truth of who you are.

When you tithe, you put God first. You are working with the *Divine Law of Prosperity*, and you cannot fail. Don't allow anyone to distract you from your commitment to create permanent, positive change in your life.

When I first began practicing these principles, I wandered around my house affirming, "I am prosperous." As I did so, my ex-spouse would follow behind, mimicking me saying, "I am preposterous." I was not deterred. No matter what others may say, stand your ground.

As you wrestle with your past beliefs about tithing, and the beliefs others may have about tithing, fear not. The reality of the situation is that you are the beloved child of abundant, loving, giving Divine parents. You hold and nurture within unique talents that draw other people together. Follow your heart and help others heal. Do not allow your fears to hold you back from making the commitment to tithe. Give thanks in every area of your life. You are worth it and you deserve it.

Session 9 Questions for Discussion

1. Where have you turned down your good because you didn't want to be viewed as needy, or a charity case? Where do you view others as needy or a charity case? What would happen if you changed your perception of "charity" to the original meaning, of "doing good or causing good to be done?"

2. Where have you given in order to get something in return?

3. What everyday ways do you tithe or withhold your tithe?

4. If "ask and you shall receive is true," what is it you would want to ask for? What do you truly desire in your life? How can you build the awareness to know that you already have it?

5. What unwanted consequences are you afraid will come with the things you ask for? How can you reframe your requests to be perfectly clear about what you want and release anxiety about not having what you want? For example, if you want a new car and you don't know how you will afford the payments, what would happen if you said, *"I want a new car AND I see all financial details regarding this new car worked out easily and effortlessly."*?

6. What intentions in the book resonated with you? How could you personalize the intentions to create what you want in your life?

7. What changes have you noticed in the way you view events that occur in your life, since you started this course?

8. How has your attitude toward past events changed since you found something to be thankful for about these past events?

9. Review your intention, report on your progress of what you're now seeing and make any changes to your intentions and those of others in your group.

10. Share some of the prosperity success stories you've experienced, and how you've tithed in all seven ways: money, thoughts, words, actions, time, efforts and possessions.

Session 9 Activities (do one or more after Session 9)

1. Practice viewing charity as it was originally known, as a way to do good or cause good to be done, both as a giver and as a receiver.

2. Practice giving out of gratitude, and just for the sheer joy of giving, with absolutely no expectation of gaining anything in return.

3. When you feel uncomfortable with something someone wants to give you or do for you, stop yourself from turning down your good and ask *"Are you sure?"* This lets the giver assess whether they are truly comfortable giving what they are giving and prevents you from assuming that they are giving "too much." If the other person says *"yes,"* then say *"thank you"* and graciously accept their tithe so that all may prosper.

4. Write out 25 times a day: "I AM Outrageous Abundance—it's my Divine Nature."

5. Write out words of praise and gratitude for different areas of your life. Praise your home, your car, your relationships, your cash flow, your health, etc. *My [blank] is amazing and I am so thankful for it.*

6. Write down your desire for yourself in the form of an intention. See yourself recognizing you already have what you desire. See yourself *knowing* that this desire has manifested in your life in ways that are *always* for your highest good.

7. Continue to write down the forward motion that occurs toward your desires, so you see how everything you give with gratitude moves you into awareness of your desire's presence.

8. Continue your gift recording journal, assigning a monetary value to everything you receive.

9. Give something away to someone every day.

10. Hold each person's intention in prayer.

11. Watch your language.

12. Use a fresh *Prosperity Tracker* to track the good that comes to you.

Now that you've completed Session 9, begin tithing 9%

Chapter Ten

Before Session 10:
- Read Chapter 10

During Session 10:
- Discuss your experience doing the activities after Session 9
- Discuss the questions at the end of Chapter 10
- Do at least one activity listed at the end of this chapter

After Session 10:
- Begin tithing 10%
- Do the remaining activities listed at the end of this chapter

Every Ending is a
New Beginning

It is my fervent hope that this book has helped you gain a spiritual understanding of tithing as well as an intellectual understanding.

Knowing that tithing works, and *believing* you are giving thanks for the abundant good in your life when you tithe, are two distinct entities.

Many people ask me why tithing works in the context I present. They want to know why tithing work on a deeper level.

Tithing works because tithing aligns you with unconditional giving. The act of giving thanks aligns you with the positive universal energy within you. Tithing is about letting go of your attachments. It's about releasing instead of grasping. Tithing opens you up to receive and experience the Allness, the Fullness of Life.

Giving and receiving aren't opposite sides of the same coin or even different parts of a continuum or cycle. Giving and receiving are actually one and the same thing. Hence the well-worn phrase: *As you give, so shall you receive.*

Tithing gives you an opportunity to examine all the ways you give with attachment—so you can practice and work through and release those attachments. When you are no longer focused on getting—when you stop trying to *get* something you desire, when you finally surrender that illusion of control—you open up unexpected channels that allow that good to come to you.

You become part of a chain reaction of positive energy, simply by giving thanks.

As a result, you discover truly and deeply, Divine Love IN you, AS you, IS you! The Divine Love you *are*, blesses and multiplies all that you *are*, all that you *do*, all that you *give* and all that you *experience*.

Whether you tithe with your money, time, actions, words or thoughts, everyone you touch with that tithe is changed. They receive your tithe and find themselves inexplicably tithing themselves in ways that go way beyond giving financially.

Take the time to smile at a harried mother at the mall, help an older gentleman find something at the grocery store, let someone into traffic, leave an extra-large tip for an exhausted but attentive waitress. All of these are ways of tithing. Tithing is a universal law of motion.

Isaac Newton's first law of motion, commonly called the Law of Inertia states: "An object at rest tends to stay at rest and an object in motion tends to stay in motion with the same speed and in the same direction unless acted upon by an outside force." This simple law is why tithing works in the context shared in this book.

I invite you to repeat this program. Explore questions that come up and write or email me. My intention is to help you raise your prosperity consciousness to a new level, so you can truly create the life you desire. I welcome your feedback and I love hearing how tithing changes *your* life!

I cannot take you into the land of spiritual understanding where your abundance awaits you. I can, however, tell you how to seek this land and I can even relate story after story of the treasures others have found in this land.

But you must undertake the journey for yourself.

You must step out in faith and prime your own pump.

I have given you all the tools you need. I have shown you the pump and provided you with a heaping helping of spiritual food. Use the spiritual inspiration contained in this book as your first cup of water to prime the pump. The rest is up to you.

For ongoing inspiration, I encourage you to visit my website (www.paulalangguthryan.com) and subscribe to my free newsletter. While you are there, take advantage of the other free (and low-cost) resources we offer.

You must find the courage to do what you think you cannot do, as Eleanor Roosevelt would say.

I wish you well on your journey, my friend.

—Paula Langguth Ryan

P.S. Please write and let me know how your life is unfolding for your highest good. I love receiving cards, letters, postcards and photographs from my readers. Correspondence, tithes and offerings can be sent to support our ministry at:

Paula Langguth Ryan*

PO Box 7530, Denver, CO 80207

www.PaulaLangguthRyan.com

*For tax-deductible tithes, please make your check out to The Village Gathering, or tithe online at http://thevillagegathering.com

Session 10 Questions for Discussion

1. How does it feel to be tithing a full 10% financially this week?

2. How would you react if you suddenly found your income doubling this month? Who would your ego want to say a big "so there!" to?

3. What would you do with your newfound income? What would you create?

4. How would you change?

5. How would you react if you suddenly realized you have everything you ever wanted, right now, and all your needs and desires are fulfilled instantly?

6. How strong are your values? Where can you start working to strengthen your values?

7. What scarcity models of life are you still choosing to hang onto?

8. What other shoe are you waiting to drop?

9. During the past nine sessions, how have you expanded your feelings about abundance beyond anything that you could possibly have imagined for yourself before today?

10. What guidance have you received since Session 9? Which guidance have you taken action on? Which guidance have you ignored so far? Why did you take action or ignore the guidance you were given?

11. What steps can you take right now to be ready to visibly accept what it is you say you truly want in your life? Where can you "prepare the way"?

Session 10 Activities (do one in class and the others on your own after Session 10)

1. Hold your breath as long as you can. Feel how deeply and purely air goes rushing into your lungs when you finally stop withholding and impeding the flow of good. Hold your breath again, as long as you can. When you breathe in again, envision the air that comes in as the unimpeded flow of abundance that you *are*, with every breath you take. Take five minutes every day to breathe in as deeply as you can, to remind yourself of your connection to abundant flow.

2. Bless everything in your life, especially all things financial. When you sit down and write out your bills, or pay someone for anything, spend a moment to think about what the money you're spending actually represents. Give thanks for what you've received. Then joyfully exchange your financial energy for what you have received already. See all money you send out as an investment in yourself, your future, and your world.

3. Turn tithing into an active game of thanksgiving. Actively seek out people who feed your spirit and tithe to them. Look for times you smile or chuckle over something you see, read or hear and immediately ask yourself: *Who can I thank for this gift?*

4. Make a list of all the people, things, debts, situations and attachments to outcomes in your life or in your past that no longer serve you. Circle any you are willing to release.

5. Be mindful of where you focus your attention. Do you focus on the cash flow (appearances) or do you focus on the bigger picture (perceiving your desires as visible)?

Now that you've completed Session 10, begin tithing 10%

Prosperity Tracker

For: _____

Dates: _____

Money				
Creative/Inspired Ideas				
Gifts				
Wisdom/Guidance				
Improved Relationships				
Increased Health				
Customers/Clients/ Contracts/Work Events				
Opportunities/Savings/ Deals/Reduced Expenses				
Freedom				
Peace of Mind				
Protection From Harm				
Kindness From Others				

Abundance
Zapping Words

12 Simple Words and Phrases to Eliminate From Your Vocabulary to See Instant Abundant Results In Your Life

1. BUT—substitute with AND
2. TRY—substitute with AM or DO
3. WORKING ON—substitute with AM or DO
4. GOING TO—substitute with AM or I SEE MYSELF
5. ATTEMPTING TO—substitute with AM or DO
6. SHOULD—substitute with GET TO or WANT TO
7. HAVE TO—substitute with GET TO or WANT TO
8. NEED TO—substitute with GET TO or WANT TO
9. CAN'T—substitute with DON'T WANT TO
10. NEVER—substitute with IN THE PAST
11. ALWAYS—substitute with IN THE PAST
12. IF—substitute with WHEN

Additional Phrases to Eliminate From Your Vocabulary

1. I CAN'T AFFORD: substitute with THAT'S NOT WHERE I'M ALLOCATING MY FUNDS; or I'VE ALREADY ALLOCATED MY FUNDS or THAT'S NOT WHERE I CHOOSE TO SPEND MY MONEY TODAY

2. COSTS TOO MUCH: substitute with I'M NOT INTERESTED IN PAYING THAT MUCH or THAT'S NOT HOW I CHOOSE TO SPEND MY MONEY TODAY

3. CAN'T MAKE IT or CAN'T DO IT: substitute with I'LL BE THERE IN SPIRIT or I'VE MADE OTHER PLANS or THAT'S NOT HOW I CHOOSE TO SPEND MY TIME TODAY

4. I HAVE TO GO or I HAVE TO DO: substitute with I CHOOSE TO or I WANT TO or I GET TO or I AM FREE TO

Additional Notes

Acknowledgments

First and foremost, I thank God—"the God of My Understanding"—the indwelling Christ Spirit, Divine Love, for all the incredible gifts in my life, especially the gift of courage. You were right: I'm not sure I do have a big enough container to hold it all. But day by day I'm learning to *be* a bigger container.

As always, an entire community helped support my work and this project with tithes of their time, talent, treasures and spirit.

Ginormous thanks to Rachelle Gardner, whose guidance and insights for the inclusion of the study guide truly created order out of chaos.

My eternal gratitude to: Refik Agri, Sue Bailey, Linda Damesyn, Robert Drake, Janet and Robbie Hall, Nellie Lauth, April J. May, Luanne McKenna, Kathy Miller, Kaye and Jervais Phillips, Shirley Proctor, Marty Ward and Ted Zeiders. If I've overlooked anyone, it's not for lack of love.

I offer my heartfelt thanks to all my coaching clients, *A Course in Miracles* fellow travelers, event attendees, newsletter subscribers, readers and others who have sought answers to their questions about how we can learn to acknowledge and accept our divine birthright of Universal Abundance. Your questions were as valuable to me as your more tangible support.

Special thanks to my original Monday night prosperity class (hugs to Anita, Amy, April, Edith, Linda, Mary and Pat) for being such willing guinea pigs, for trusting the process and for all your love and support.

A big woof of thanks (again) to my fellow spiritual traveler Linda Damesyn for being the best friend, dancing buddy and dog-sitter a girl could ever ask for. My unending love and appreciation to April J. May and Julie Hall Runion for being willing students, believing in my work without fail and being the most enthusiastic voluntary publicists in the world.

Special thanks to Rev. Catherine Ponder for introducing me to the art of tithing and for graciously writing the Foreword to this book; to Rev. Judith Elia for being my first prosperity penpal and for becoming my treasured friend; to Beth Kaufman for teaching me the importance of living an authentic life; to Kaye Phillips for reminding me that nothing is ever truly lost or destroyed; to Diane Scribner Clevenger for reminding me to laugh; and to Nellie Lauth, for just being.

Endless gratitude to Sarah Porter, whose tenacity, creativity, skill set and hearty agreement to my crazy projects *always* makes me look good.

Above all else, my heartfelt gratitude and love to my beloved family: Sandy and Cooper. You are my heart and home.

Thank you all for being exactly who you are.

About the Author

Paula Langguth Ryan is an Independent Unity Minister, an internationally renowned communications facilitator, conflict resolution consultant and keynote speaker, specializing in helping people recognize and resolve conflicts with compassion and clarity. Her daily *Conflict Free Zone* radio aired worldwide for two years and her "21 Days to a More Abundant Life," "Break the Debt Cycle—For Good!" and "Know Your True Worth" workshops have transformed thousands of lives.

As a communication facilitator, Ryan has worked with individuals, couples, families, small groups and large communities in 10 countries to create positive outcomes. Her "Ryan's Rules of Order" is a guideline for sustainable success in a multitude of diverse settings.

Ryan is the author of *Manifest the Perfect Mate, Bounce Back From Bankruptcy* and co-author of *Effortless Freedom from Clutter and Debt*. She has been featured extensively in national media.

An amateur juggler and semi-professional harmonica player, Ryan lives in Colorado with her beloved, her son and their Irish Wolfhound, where they all practice these principles on a daily basis—even when egos would prefer otherwise!

Visit her website for more details and information.

www.PaulaLangguthRyan.com

Other Tools

by Paula Langguth Ryan

Services

Paula offers customized keynote speeches, leadership training, empowerment seminars/workshops, conflict resolution services, communication skills consulting, debt negotiation, and mediation services for individuals, organizations, and corporations. Visit her website to get on Paula's calendar or discuss booking her for an event.

Audio/CD/Workbook Sets
- 21 Days to a More Abundant Life
- Break the Debt Cycle—for Good!
- The Right and Perfect Series: How to Manifest the Right and Perfect Job, Clients, Mate, and Home Buyer

Publications
- *Manifest the Perfect Mate*
- *Bounce Back from Bankruptcy: A Step-by-Step Guide to Getting Back on Your Financial Feet*
- *Heal Your Relationship with Money*
- *Feng Shui Bagua Vision Treasure Mapping Playkit*
- *Effortless Freedom from Clutter and Debt*

Please add a short review on Amazon
and let me know what you thought!